First World War
and Army of Occupation
War Diary
France, Belgium and Germany

19 DIVISION
56 Infantry Brigade,
Brigade Trench Mortar Battery
4 February 1916 - 31 December 1918

WO95/2082/3

The Naval & Military Press Ltd
www.nmarchive.com
Published in association with The National Archives

Published by

The Naval & Military Press Ltd

Unit 10 Ridgewood Industrial Park,
Uckfield, East Sussex,
TN22 5QE England
Tel: +44 (0) 1825 749494

www.naval-military-press.com

www.nmarchive.com

This diary has been reprinted in facsimile from the original. Any imperfections are inevitably reproduced and the quality may fall short of modern type and cartographic standards.

© Crown Copyright
Images reproduced by permission of The National Archives, London, England, 2015.

Contents

Document type	Place/Title	Date From	Date To
Heading	WO95/2082-3		
Heading	56th Trench Mortar Bty 1916 Feb Nov 1918		
Heading	19 Div 56 Bde 56 Trench Mortar Bty 1916 Feb To 1916 Mar		
War Diary	Le Touquet Berthe	04/02/1916	05/02/1916
War Diary	Laucashire Support Farm	06/02/1916	04/03/1916
Heading	War Diary Of 56 Trench Mortar Battery From 1st September 1917 To 30th September 1917		
War Diary	Mont Vidaigne	01/09/1917	01/09/1917
War Diary	Westoutre	05/09/1917	06/09/1917
War Diary	Locre	06/09/1917	19/09/1917
War Diary	Bois Carre	19/09/1917	21/09/1917
War Diary	Hill 60	21/09/1917	29/09/1917
War Diary	Kemmel	30/09/1917	05/11/1917
War Diary	Shrewsbury Forest	05/11/1917	14/11/1917
War Diary	Kleine Vierstraat	14/11/1917	14/11/1917
War Diary	Kemmel	19/11/1917	27/11/1917
War Diary	Line	27/11/1917	30/11/1917
Heading	War Diary Of 56 Trench Mortar Battery From 1 XI 1917 To 30 XI 1917		
War Diary	Line	01/11/1917	04/11/1917
War Diary	Kemmel	05/11/1917	10/11/1917
War Diary	Wallon Capell	11/11/1917	30/11/1917
War Diary	Wallon Capell	01/12/1917	06/12/1917
War Diary	Bailleulmont	06/12/1917	07/12/1917
War Diary	Courcelles Le Comte	08/12/1917	08/12/1917
War Diary	Etricourt	09/12/1917	12/12/1917
War Diary	Line	12/12/1917	16/12/1917
War Diary	Ribecourt	19/12/1917	28/12/1917
War Diary	Haurincourt Wood	28/12/1917	31/12/1917
Miscellaneous	To 56th Infantry Brigade	31/01/1918	31/01/1918
War Diary	Haurincourt Wood	01/01/1918	03/01/1918
War Diary	Highland Ridge Line	03/01/1918	12/01/1918
War Diary	Haurincourt Wood	12/01/1918	12/01/1918
War Diary	Line	17/01/1918	29/01/1918
War Diary	Havrincourt Wood	30/01/1918	30/01/1918
Heading	19th Division. 56th Infantry Brigade 56th Light Trench Mortar Battery March 1918		
War Diary	Bouzincourt	01/03/1918	07/03/1918
War Diary	Le Transloy	07/03/1918	21/03/1918
War Diary	Velu	21/03/1918	21/03/1918
War Diary	Beugny	21/03/1918	21/03/1918
War Diary	Fremicourt	22/03/1918	24/03/1918
War Diary	Bapaume	24/03/1918	24/03/1918
War Diary	Grevillers	25/03/1918	25/03/1918
War Diary	Henu	28/03/1918	28/03/1918
War Diary	Famechon	29/03/1918	29/03/1918
War Diary	Kemmel	30/03/1918	31/03/1918
War Diary	Bouzincourt	01/03/1918	09/03/1918
War Diary	Le Transloy	17/03/1918	21/03/1918

War Diary	Velu	21/03/1918	21/03/1918
War Diary	Beugny	21/03/1918	21/03/1918
War Diary	Fremicourt	22/03/1918	24/03/1918
War Diary	Bapaume	24/03/1918	24/03/1918
War Diary	Grevillers	25/03/1918	25/03/1918
War Diary	Henu	28/03/1918	28/03/1918
War Diary	Famechon	29/03/1918	29/03/1918
War Diary	Kemmel	30/03/1918	31/03/1918
Heading	56th Light Trench Mortar Battery April 1918.		
War Diary	Lindenhoek	01/04/1918	02/04/1918
War Diary	Wulverghem	03/04/1918	10/04/1918
War Diary	Neuve Eglise	10/04/1918	10/04/1918
War Diary	Hill 63	10/04/1918	11/04/1918
War Diary	Dranoutre	12/04/1918	12/04/1918
War Diary	Westoutre	12/04/1918	15/04/1918
War Diary	Kemmel	15/04/1918	16/04/1918
War Diary	Scherpenberg	16/04/1918	19/04/1918
War Diary	Wippenhoek	19/04/1918	20/04/1918
War Diary	St Janter Biezen	21/04/1918	25/04/1918
War Diary	Ouderdom	26/04/1918	30/04/1918
War Diary	Lindenhoek	01/04/1918	02/04/1918
War Diary	Wulverghem	03/04/1918	10/04/1918
War Diary	Neuve Eglise	10/04/1918	10/04/1918
War Diary	Hill 63.	10/04/1918	11/04/1918
War Diary	Dranoutre	12/04/1918	12/04/1918
War Diary	Westoutre	12/04/1918	15/04/1918
War Diary	Kemmel	15/04/1918	16/04/1918
War Diary	Scherpenberg	16/04/1918	19/04/1918
War Diary	Wippenhoek	19/04/1918	20/04/1918
War Diary	St Janter Biezen	21/04/1918	25/04/1918
War Diary	Ouderdom	26/04/1918	30/04/1918
War Diary	Ouderdom	01/05/1918	01/05/1918
War Diary	Dickebusch	02/05/1918	05/05/1918
War Diary	St. Jan-Ter-Biezen.	06/05/1918	17/05/1918
War Diary	Vitry-La Ville	18/05/1918	18/05/1918
War Diary	La Chaussee-Sur-Marne	19/05/1918	29/05/1918
War Diary	Chambrecy Pourcy	30/05/1918	30/05/1918
War Diary	Pourcy	31/05/1918	31/05/1918
War Diary	Nanteuil La Fosse	31/05/1918	31/05/1918
War Diary	Ourderdom	01/05/1918	01/05/1918
War Diary	Dickebusch	02/05/1918	05/05/1918
War Diary	St Jan-Ter-Biezen	06/05/1918	17/05/1918
War Diary	Vitry-La Ville	18/05/1918	18/05/1918
War Diary	La Chaussee Sur-Marne	19/05/1918	29/05/1918
War Diary	Chambrecy Pourcy	30/05/1918	30/05/1918
War Diary	Pourcy	31/05/1918	31/05/1918
War Diary	Nanteuil La Fusse	31/05/1918	31/05/1918
War Diary	Chaumuzy	01/06/1918	06/06/1918
War Diary	Bois De Courton	07/06/1918	21/06/1918
War Diary	Relves	21/06/1918	30/06/1918
War Diary	Broussy-Le-Grand	01/07/1918	02/07/1918
War Diary	Ruisseauville	04/07/1918	05/07/1918
War Diary	Ergny	05/07/1918	13/07/1918
War Diary	Ammettes	14/07/1918	31/07/1918
Miscellaneous	To 56 Infantry Bde	03/10/1918	03/10/1918
War Diary	Amettes	01/08/1918	06/08/1918

War Diary	Locon Sector	06/08/1918	29/08/1918
War Diary	St Sauveur	30/08/1918	31/08/1918
War Diary	Amettes	01/08/1918	06/08/1918
War Diary	Locon Sector	06/08/1918	29/08/1918
War Diary	St Sauveur	30/08/1918	31/08/1918
War Diary	St Sauveur	01/09/1918	16/09/1918
War Diary	Bas Annezin	18/09/1918	19/09/1918
War Diary	Bomy	20/09/1918	02/10/1918
War Diary	Raimbert	03/10/1918	04/10/1918
War Diary	Saulty	05/10/1918	08/10/1918
War Diary	Graincourt	09/10/1918	12/10/1918
War Diary	Cambrai	13/10/1918	19/10/1918
War Diary	St Aubert	20/10/1918	26/10/1918
War Diary	Cagnoncles	27/10/1918	31/10/1918
War Diary		01/10/1918	02/10/1918
War Diary	Raimbert	03/10/1918	04/10/1918
War Diary	Saulty	05/10/1918	08/10/1918
War Diary	Graincourt	09/10/1918	12/10/1918
War Diary	Cambrai	13/10/1918	19/10/1918
War Diary	St Aubert	20/10/1918	26/10/1918
War Diary	Cagnoncles	27/10/1918	31/10/1918
Operation(al) Order(s)	56th Infantry Brigade Operation Order No. 161.	19/10/1918	19/10/1918
Miscellaneous	56th Infantry Brigade Administrative Instructions No. 32	19/10/1918	19/10/1918
Heading	Vol 41 November 18		
Heading	Headquarters 19th Division		
Heading	To 56 Infantry 18 Bde	02/12/1918	02/12/1918
War Diary		01/11/1918	01/11/1918
War Diary	Artres	02/11/1918	02/11/1918
War Diary	Mareshes	03/11/1918	03/11/1918
War Diary	Jenlain	04/11/1918	04/11/1918
War Diary	Wargnies-Le-Grand	04/11/1918	04/11/1918
War Diary	Taisniere	10/11/1918	10/11/1918
War Diary	Bry	11/11/1918	15/11/1918
War Diary	Rieux	15/11/1918	25/11/1918
War Diary	Cambrai	26/11/1918	28/11/1918
War Diary	Talmas	29/11/1918	30/11/1918
War Diary	Wargnies-Le-Grand	04/11/1918	04/11/1918
War Diary	Bry	05/11/1918	05/11/1918
War Diary	Flamengrie	05/11/1918	08/11/1918
War Diary	Taisniere	08/11/1918	09/11/1918
War Diary		01/11/1918	01/11/1918
War Diary	Artres	02/11/1918	02/11/1918
War Diary	Mareshes	03/11/1918	03/11/1918
War Diary	Jenlain	04/11/1918	04/11/1918
War Diary	Wargnies Le-Grand	04/11/1918	04/11/1918
War Diary	Bry	05/11/1918	05/11/1918
War Diary	Flamengrie	05/11/1918	08/11/1918
War Diary	Taisniere	09/11/1918	10/11/1918
War Diary	Bry	11/11/1918	15/11/1918
War Diary	Rieux	15/11/1918	25/11/1918
War Diary	Cambrai	26/11/1918	28/11/1918
War Diary	Talmas	29/11/1918	11/12/1918
War Diary	Villers	12/12/1918	12/12/1918
War Diary	L'Hopital	12/12/1918	31/12/1918

WO 95/2082/3

19TH DIVISION
56TH INFY BDE

56TH TRENCH MORTAR BTY

1916 FEB ~~SEP 1917~~ - NOV 1918

19TH DIVISION
56TH INFY BDE

~~Army Troops~~

19 DIV 56 Bde

56 TRENCH MORTAR BTY

1916 FEB to 1916 MAR

(1805)

Army Form C. 2118

WAR DIARY or INTELLIGENCE SUMMARY

58th T.M.

(Erase heading not required.)

H.Q. Place	Date	Hour	Summary of Events and Information	Remarks and references to Appendices
Tongue Butt	4/2/16	5.15 p.m.	58th T.M. Battery arrived at La Tongue Butte & billeted at Vice Regal Vice Regal Lodge.	
"	5/2/16		Visited H.Q. 11th Royal Scots for purpose of obtaining accommodation in my line. Unsuccessful. Visited H.Q. 6th R.S. Fusiliers for some purpose & allotted 1 officer & Dugout to dug out for 8 men at Lancashire Support Farm. Officer & half the personnel move into Lancashire Support Farm. Remainder with Cpl Crawford remain at Vice regal Lodge.	
Lancashire Support Farm	6/2/16		Brig-Gen Ritchie, & Major Gordon 6th R.S.F. gave me some valuable help in completing arrangements for accommodation. Whole personnel with guns & stores billet in Lancashire Support Farm.	
"	7/2/16		Visited 11th Royal Scots in morning to gain knowledge of the line. Men on gun drill & cleaning quarters.	
"	8/2/16		Visited St Yves to make reconnaissance for a short time on 10/2/16. Men on gun drill & cleaning equipment etc.	
"	9/2/16		Built temporary emplacements at St Yves at U.15.D.4.7½, – U.15 D.4½ 5½, – U.15.D.4.4½ & U.15 D.5.8½.	
"	10/2/16		Shoot at St Yves. 70 rounds fired. Nil Casualties.	
"	11/2/16		Went round battalion.	
"	12/2/16		The battery covey to which the Battery was sent took 2 hours of deliberation started construction of a defensive emplacement in communication trench 115 yds from Convent. Battery relieved. Two men sent to get you to bring back further knowledge.	
"	13/2/16		Work on emplacement hampered by rain.	
"	14/2/16		Shoot from Burnt out farm. 30 rounds fired from U.28.A.33. Only enemy's trench at U.28.A.3.?. Casualties Nil.	
"	15/2/16		Continued work on defensive emplacement. Visited all Coy commanders on my front that H.Q.'s	
"	16/2/16		Work hampered by rain during day but considerable progress made. dfts to dark so on the defensive emplacement.	

WAR DIARY
or
INTELLIGENCE SUMMARY
(Erase heading not required.)

Army Form C. 2118

Instructions regarding War Diaries and Intelligence Summaries are contained in F.S. Regs., Part II. and the Staff Manual respectively. Title Pages will be prepared in manuscript.

Place	Date	Hour	Summary of Events and Information	Remarks and references to Appendices
Lancashire Support Farm	28/2/16		Relieved Lieut Cole. Made Reconnaissance of defensive positions with O.C. Trench Mortar Bde, 9th Div. Visited H.Q.s 6th R.S.F. & front line.	
— " —	29/2/16		Work started on dug out near Convent for 2 temporary accomodation of personnel of defensive position. R.E. stores for completing scheme arrived mid day. Indent not fully delivered — Received only 2 bags nails, 250 ft timber & sandbags. Party worked till 9 p.m. Visited H.Q. 6th R.S.F. & trench line.	
— " —	1/3/16		Work continued. Transferred 4.2.2" bombs from ferm-a-Phine Cottage to dump at rail head on Ploegsteert to Bizet road, a 19 bombs of 2" mts from same place to R.E. Dump at Le Touquet Battle. Fatigue party arrived 11.3.20 am 2/3/16. Visited H.Q. 6th R.S.F.	
— " —	2/3/16		Owing to little sleep previous night — the men had the morning off. Work continued in the afternoon. Visited Front line. 27th Bde. relieved	
— " —	3/3/16		Men cleaned guns & parts. Visited H.Q. 8th R. Highlanders & front line. Then working on defensive emplacement. Sent party down to cover the bombs at Le Touquet Battle. R.E. advise that 18 Dug out frame is ready. Party dispatched to fetch same. H.Q. 8th Gordons too busy to see me today.	
— " —	4/3/16		Snowing heavily. Work impossible. Battery relieved.	

R.A. Dalrymple
O/c 57th T.M.B.
4/3/16

CONFIDENTIAL

War Diary.

of

56 Trench Mortar Battery.

from 1st September 1917 to 30th September 1917.

Nov 18

WAR DIARY
or
INTELLIGENCE SUMMARY

Army Form C. 2118.

Place	Date	Hour	Summary of Events and Information	Remarks and references to Appendices
MONT VIDAIGNE	1/9/17 to		Battery in Camp in IX Corps Reserve area. Training carried out. Verbal particulars of attacks being given of the area gun drill adopted by Field Battery. On 1st inst the form of drill was submitted to Brigade and statement (where approval received)	
WESTOUTRE	5/9/17		Then, in turn, sent of to 6th Division who had their permission for the men in the unit	
	6/9/17		Proc: to LOCRE area and billets in BIRR BARRACKS	
LOCRE	6/9/17 to 19/9/17		Battery billets in BIRR BARRACKS, LOCRE training and (employed) on working parties	
BOIS CARRÉ	19/9/17 to 21/9/17		Battery moved from LOCRE during the evening of 19th inst to BOIS CARRÉ where it was in Divisional Reserve for the attack on 20th. Remained there until the evening of 21st.	
HILL 60	21/9/17 to		Took over Head Quarters at HILL 60 from 57 T.M.By. Also took over the guns of 58 T.M.By. on the line. Six Stokes mortars in the line, three in Left Battalion of Divisional front near BELGIAN WOOD, and two in right Battalion near HOLLEBEKE CHATEAU. On 24th inst the three mortars on the Left were withdrawn under Brigade Orders and the Headquarters of the Battery moved to SPOIL BANK. Battery relieved on night of 29th inst by 58 T.M.By.	
KEMMEL	30/9/17		Battery H.Qrs. established at KEMMEL on night of 29th after relief by 58 T.M.By.	

Army Form C. 2118.

WAR DIARY
of
INTELLIGENCE SUMMARY.
(Erase heading not required.)

56 TMB

Place	Date	Hour	Summary of Events and Information	Remarks and references to Appendices
KEMMEL	1/4/17		Battn in ROSSIGNOL CAMP and KEMMEL Shelters	
KRUISTRAAT FOREST	5/4/17		Battn relieved 91 T.M.B. in the line. Bttn HQrs nr KRUISTRAAT FOREST	
			Battn reads. At posts improved by men. G.O.S. inflated into air if wind [illegible]	
			E.S.W. Two A.P.N. [illegible]	
		10/4/17	Relieved in the line by 97 T.M.B. 69 T.M. [illegible]	
KLEINE VIERSTRAAT	11/4/17		Battn in rest at KLEINE VIERSTRAAT. In [illegible]	
			Working parts for R.E.	
KEMMEL	18/4/17 to 21/4/17		Battn (less trans) to ROSSIGNOL CAMP. A train programme of Musky [illegible] carried out	
	22/4/17		Relieved 55 T.M.B. in the line. H.Qrs when Bttn established in STOCK BANK. Two [illegible]	
LINE	29/4/17		Guns in the line. Not firing for a week for the night of the 28th inst.	
	30/4/17		[illegible signature] [illegible] Bty.	

CONFIDENTIAL

WAR DIARY

of

56 Trench Mortar Battery

From 1.XI.1917 To 30.XI.1917

Army Form C. 2118.

WAR DIARY
or
INTELLIGENCE SUMMARY.
(Erase heading not required.)

Instructions regarding War Diaries and Intelligence Summaries are contained in F. S. Regs, Part II. and the Staff Manual respectively. Title pages will be prepared in manuscript.

Place	Date	Hour	Summary of Events and Information	Remarks and references to Appendices
LINE	1/11/17		Battery was in action in the line. Head Quarters were in THE SPOIL BANK near ST ELOI. Three guns were in the bar. Fifty seven rounds were fired during the night	
	2/11/17		on hostile posts.	
			No.215195 Cpl HILL. S. 7th East Lanc. Regt. (attached) 56 T.M. B'y and No. 14070 Cpl CRANKSHAW. D. 7th East Lanc. Regt. attached 56 T.M. B'y were presented with medal ribbons (Military Medals awarded 4.9.17 - 4/11/17) by G.O.C. XIX Division	
	3/11/17		Thirty three rounds were fired during the night of 3/11/17 - 4/11/17 on hostile posts. A dart was attached on an Enemy T.M. position	
	4/11/17		(Lihous) in the line by 57 T.M. B'y and (?)	Kenna
KEMMEL	5/11/17 to 7/11/17		A daily programme of Training was carried out.	
	8/11/17		The Battery left Rossignol Camp and proceeded by route march to BIRR BARRACKS at LOCRE.	
	9/11/17		The Battery left BIRR BARRACKS & proceeded by route march to N°4	

Army Form C. 2118.

WAR DIARY
or
INTELLIGENCE SUMMARY.
(Erase heading not required.)

Place	Date	Hour	Summary of Events and Information	Remarks and references to Appendices
	10/11/17		CAMP on the MONT NOIR area	
			The Battery left NOH CAMP and proceeded by road march to BAILEUL thence by train to EBBLINGHAM and thence by route march to billets at WALLON CAPELL	
WALLON CAPELL	11/11/17 to 30/11/17		A daily programme of Training carried out. Shoeing, physical drill, harness cleaning, attack team pair to the elements of Heavy Infantry Training, Pioneer & Signal duty. Both Artillery & Infantry Special personnel has been made for the newly attached personnel to learn in every detail the use of the above Arms.	[signature]

J. T. House Capt
OC 56 F.N. Bty

Army Form C. 2118.

WAR DIARY
or
INTELLIGENCE SUMMARY.
(Erase heading not required.)

Instructions regarding War Diaries and Intelligence Summaries are contained in F. S. Regs., Part II. and the Staff Manual respectively. Title pages will be prepared in manuscript.

Place	Date	Hour	Summary of Events and Information	Remarks and references to Appendices
WALLON CAPELL	1/12/17 to 6/12/17		Battery in billets near WALLON CAPELL. A daily programme of training in Stable Routine, Bayonet fighting, musketry etc. was carried out	
BAILLEULMONT	6/12/17 7.12.17		Battery left billets at 3 a.m. and proceeded by march route to STEEN BECQUE. Entrained and proceeded via LILLERS, ST. POL, FREVENT, DOULLENS, to SAULTY on the DOULLENS/ARRAS Road. Proceeded by march route to the village of BAILLEULMONT and spent the night in billets there. The 19th Divisional Arty. forms part of VII Corps. in the III Army.	
COURCELLES LE COMTE	8.12.17		Left billets at 1 p.m. and proceeded by march route via ADINFER to COURCELLES LE COMTE and billeted there for the night.	
ETRICOURT	9.12.17 to 12.12.17		Left billets at 8 a.m. and proceeded by march route via ACHIET-LE-GRAND, BAPAUME, LE TRANSLOY to a camp near the village of ETRICOURT. Remainder of time until the afternoon of 12th inst. was being spent in Stationary camp and in musketry training.	

WAR DIARY or INTELLIGENCE SUMMARY

Army Form C. 2118.

Place	Date	Hour	Summary of Events and Information	Remarks and references to Appendices
LINE	12.12.17		Left billets at 2pm and proceeded to trenches in Reserve Brigade area as infantry, forming a part of 7th East Lanc. Regt. Battery occupied a portion of the old HINDENBURG SUPPORT TRENCH. 19th Division in III Corps.	
do.	15.12.17		Relieved 57. T.B. B'y in the left section of 19th Divisional line. Took over four guns in the line and established Battery H.Q's in the village of RIBECOURT. Transferred to IV Corps.	
do.	16.12.17		Battery suffered [illegible] ...	
RIBECOURT	19.12.17 8pm		...	
HAVRINCOURT WOOD			... at HAVRINCOURT WOOD ...	

> 56TH
> TRENCH MORTAR
> BATTERY
>
> No ....
> Date 31.1.18

To
56th Infantry Brigade

Battery War Diary for January herewith
Please acknowledge receipt.

J. Hoare
Capt
O.C. 56 T.M.B.

Army Form C. 2118.

WAR DIARY
or
INTELLIGENCE SUMMARY.
(Erase heading not required.)

Instructions regarding War Diaries and Intelligence Summaries are contained in F.S. Regs., Part II. and the Staff Manual respectively. Title pages will be prepared in manuscript.

Place	Date	Hour	Summary of Events and Information	Remarks and references to Appendices
HAVRINCOURT WOOD	1/1/18 to 3/1/18		In camp at HAVRINCOURT WOOD. Brigade being in Divisional Reserve.	
HIGHLAND RIDGE LINE	3/1/18		Relieved the 190 Brigade (Naval Division) T.M.B. on the WELSH RIDGE and the HIGHLAND RIDGE took over three guns in the line and established Battery Head Quarters in WOOD SUPPORT.	
do	3/1/18 to 11/1/18		In the line - constructed six new emplacements, the targets being exceptionally good. Consisting in every case of hostile posts, machine gun or bombing. On the nights of 6-7, 8-9 the Battery put up a protective barrage in support of wiring parties of the 9/10 Kings Own Royal Lancaster Regiment. The barrage was effective in keeping down hostile machine gun fire & the working parties had no casualties.	
	11/1/18		Relieved by 57 T.M.B. - handed over seven guns in the line.	

Army Form C. 2118.

WAR DIARY
or
INTELLIGENCE SUMMARY.
(Erase heading not required.)

Place	Date	Hour	Summary of Events and Information	Remarks and references to Appendices
HAVRINCOURT WOOD	11/2/1/18		The Battery proceeded out of the line to HAWES CAMP in HAVRINCOURT WOOD the Brigade having become Divisional Reserve.	
LINE.	17/1/18		The Battery left the WOOD and proceeded to the line, took over from the 58 T.M. Battery who had 9 guns in the line, 5 being laid on S.O.S. lines. Owing to the severe nature of the thaw which had just set in, most of the emplacements had become useless. This necessitated very hard work on the part of the Battery, who at once commenced to sandbag them & make them generally serviceable. Firing once begun, was carried out with consistency and energy, the principal targets being hostile machine gun posts and light T.M. Emplacements.	
do	24/1/18		The principle of firing gun away from a regular emplacement, was first adopted. A gun was set up immediately behind the front line fired 5 rounds & then withdrawn, retaliation on the reported emplacement followed.	
do	27/1/18		On the night of the 27th the above principle was still further extended and a gun was carried forward to a position in the GRAND RAVINE about 200 yards in advance of our front line 25 rounds were fired, the infantry (9 W.W.) co-operating by firing rifle grenades and providing the necessary covering party. Enemy retaliated by opening machine guns on the firing party.	

Army Form C. 2118.

WAR DIARY
or
INTELLIGENCE SUMMARY.

(Erase heading not required.)

Place	Date	Hour	Summary of Events and Information	Remarks and references to Appendices
LINE	28/1/18 29/1/18		On two subsequent nights a similar scheme was carried out. The guns being switched to Area, retaliation almost invariably following on the regular emplacements which are visible in aeroplane photographs	
HAVRINCOURT WOOD	30/1/18		The Battery was relieved by the 57 T.M. Bty and proceeded to the HAWES CAMP in HAVRINCOURT WOOD	

John Preston Lt
57 T.M Bty

31 January 1918.

19th Division.
56th Infantry brigade

WAR DIARY

56th LIGHT TRENCH MORTAR BATTERY

MARCH 1918

Army Form C. 2118.

WAR DIARY
or
INTELLIGENCE SUMMARY.
(Erase heading not required.)

Instructions regarding War Diaries and Intelligence Summaries are contained in F. S. Regs, Part II. and the Staff Manual respectively. Title pages will be prepared in manuscript.

Place	Date	Hour	Summary of Events and Information	Remarks and references to Appendices
	MARCH			
BOUZINCOURT	1st to 6/17		Battery in Billets in Village of Bouzincourt carrying out a programme of progressive training	
LE TRANSLOY	7th to 20th		Left BOUZINCOURT and proceeded by route march to AVELUY thence by train to BAPAUME and marched to camp on the BAPAUME - PERONNE Road near the SUCRERIE at LE TRANSLOY. In camp between BEAURENCOURT and LETRANSLOY a daily programme of training including the firing of live rounds was carried out	
VELU	21	5.30 a.m.	Orders stand by received from Brigade. Battery prepared to move at 20 minutes notice.	
		12 a.m.	Orders Move to camp received from Brigade. Battery moved to camp near VELU WOOD	
BEUGNY		11.30 p.m	and relieved 58 T.M.B who went forward with their Brigade. Battery ordered to rendezvous at DELSAUX FARM with rest of Brigade to occupy the GREEN or Army Line	
FREMICOURT	22	4 a.m.	Battery Headquarters established near FREMICOURT and four mortars dug in in GREEN line	

Army Form C. 2118.

WAR DIARY
or
INTELLIGENCE SUMMARY.
(Erase heading not required.)

Instructions regarding War Diaries and Intelligence Summaries are contained in F. S. Regs., Part II. and the Staff Manual respectively. Title pages will be prepared in manuscript.

Place	Date	Hour	Summary of Events and Information	Remarks and references to Appendices
FREMICOURT			Each gun being supplied with 25 rounds.	
	23.	11p.m.	Brigade front extended north of BAPAUME - CAMBRAI Road and orders received to put two mortars into the new sector. These guns were dug in during the night and supplied with 25 rounds each.	
			Orders received to remove the mortars from the north of BAPAUME - CAMBRAI road. OC Brigade was not to occupy that sector. Mortars were transferred to south side of the road. There were 6 guns in the GREEN or (Army) LINE between DELSAUX FARM and the BAPAUME - CAMBRAI Road. Therefore, 120 bombs were obtained in addition to those already in possession; thus each gun was supplied with 45 rounds.	
	24	11.a.m.	Enemy attacked right flank of the Brigade at DELSAUX FARM and captured the front line. No 1 gun fired several rounds at the advancing enemy and then the N.C.O in charge destroyed the barrel by means of a mills bomb and the team fell back with the infantry. No 2 gun fired 25 rounds at the advancing enemy and along with the base cap & along with his team fell back then the N.C.O in charge removed the base cap & along with his team fell back	

WAR DIARY
or
INTELLIGENCE SUMMARY.
(Erase heading not required.)

Army Form C. 2118.

Place	Date	Hour	Summary of Events and Information	Remarks and references to Appendices
	MARCH			
	24		with the Infantry. He reported to the nearest Infantry Officer (Capt PALMER) and that his team forward as infantry in the counter attack delivered when that Officer 9 CHESHIRES arrived at his gun position he found the mortar and Forrest intact and he immediately replaced the base cap and fired his remaining rounds at the retiring enemy. Having no more ammunition he brought his gun back to Battery Headquarters.	
		12 noon	Orders received that in the event of a withdrawal from the GREEN LINE being necessary Brigade should fall back to a line about 600 yards in front of BAPAUME facing due EAST. Battery Commander arranged with Brigade Commander that he should be allowed to withdraw just before the infantry so as to be able to carry out the mortars of which four remained in the line on the right. Battery Commander sent orders to Officer in charge of guns in the	
		1.50pm	Orders received for withdrawal from GREEN LINE owing to enemy's penetration line to withdraw and rendezvous at Brickyard about 500 yards EAST of BAPAUME on the BAPAUME - CAMBRAI road.	

Army Form C. 2118.

WAR DIARY
or
INTELLIGENCE SUMMARY.
(Erase heading not required.)

Instructions regarding War Diaries and Intelligence Summaries are contained in F. S. Regs., Part II. and the Staff Manual respectively. Title pages will be prepared in manuscript.

Place	Date	Hour	Summary of Events and Information	Remarks and references to Appendices
FREQUOURT	24		Before their crews reached the respective officers, the line had commenced to withdraw, so having fired their rounds three of the barrels were destroyed by bombs it having been found impossible to carry them out of the line. The fourth Mortar was carried out of the line. The teams fell back with the Infantry fighting as such.	
		4 p.m.	Battery assembled at Brickyard near BAPAUME with two guns. Casualties to this time 16 officers 20 O.R. missing.	
BAPAUME		4.30 p.m.	Having only two mortars and no ammunition for them Battery Commander reported to C.O. 9 Cheshire Regiment and placed himself and his Battery at his disposal as Infantry. Strength 2 Officers 19 O.R.	
		11 p.m.	Battery Commander ordered by the G.O.C. 56 Infantry Brigade to report to Brigade Headquarters to avoid Staff owing to the Brigade Major having become a casualty.	
GRÉVILLERS	25	9 a.m.	Remaining Battery Officer wounded. The two mortars had to be abandoned in the fighting in this line and the 13 O.R. of the Battery became merged in the 9 CHESHIRE REGT and retired fighting with them through IRLES, PUISIEUX to MERUTERNE.	

(A2001) Wt. W1721/M7093 750,000 5/17 Sch. 82 Forms/C2118/14
D. D. & L., London, E.C.

Army Form C. 2118.

WAR DIARY
or
INTELLIGENCE SUMMARY.
(Erase heading not required.)

Instructions regarding War Diaries and Intelligence Summaries are contained in F. S. Regs., Part II. and the Staff Manual respectively. Title pages will be prepared in manuscript.

Place	Date	Hour	Summary of Events and Information	Remarks and references to Appendices
HENU	28	7 a.m.	13 O.R of the Battery reported by Brigade orders to 2nd in Command of the Battery at Brigade transport lines at HENU	
	29	2 p.m.	Battery proceeded by March route to billets in FAMECHON	
FAMECHON	29.	5.30 a.m	Battery left billets and proceeded by March route to CANDAS and entrained. Due at 12 noon for the 2nd Army Area. Arrival at CAESTRE at 10 p.m. and proceeded by Motor Lorry to FUSILIER CAMP near KEMMEL arriving at 1 a.m.	
KEMMEL	30 to 31		Battery billeted in FUSILIER CAMP. 8 new motors drawn from DADOS, 19 Division to replace those lost in action. Strength of Battery 2 Officers and 37 O.R.	

J.T. Hewitt Capt
O.C. 56 T.M. B'y.

Army Form C. 2118.

58 TMB

WAR DIARY
or
INTELLIGENCE SUMMARY.
(Erase heading not required.)

Instructions regarding War Diaries and Intelligence Summaries are contained in F. S. Regs., Part II. and the Staff Manual respectively. Title pages will be prepared in manuscript.

Place	Date	Hour	Summary of Events and Information	Remarks and references to Appendices
BOUZINCOURT	March 6th		Battery in billets in village of Bouzincourt carrying out a programme of progressive training	
LE TRANSLOY	9th to 20th		Left BOUZINCOURT and proceeded by route march to AVELUY thence by train to BAPAUME and marched to camp on the BAPAUME - PERONNE Road near the SUCRERIE at LE TRANSLOY. In camp between BEAULENCOURT and LE TRANSLOY a daily programme of training including the firing of live rounds was carried out.	
	21	5.30 a.m.	Air "Stand by" received from Bde. Battery prepared to move at 20 minutes notice.	
VELU		12 a.m.	Gen. "Move to camp" received from Bde. Battery moved to camp near VELU WOOD and relieved 58 T.M.B. who went (?) with their Bde.	
BEUGNY		11:30 p.m.	Battery ordered to rendezvous at DELSAUX FARM and non f. Bryate to occupy the GREEN on Army Line	
FREMICOURT	22	4 a.m.	Battery Headquarters established near FREMICOURT and four mortars dug in in GREEN line	

WAR DIARY
or
INTELLIGENCE SUMMARY.

(Erase heading not required.)

Army Form C. 2118.

Place	Date	Hour	Summary of Events and Information	Remarks and references to Appendices
FREMICOURT	23	11 p.m.	Each gun being supplied with 25 rounds S.A.A. Brigade fired observed rounds & BAPAUME-CAMBRAI Road and Motor Transport to put two mortars into the new sector. Usage given more easy in worrying the enemy and supplied with 25 rounds each. Orders received to remove the mortars from the road and parapmnt positions and as enemy was not to occupy Ant Sector. Mortars were transferred to Gun set of the Road. There were 6 guns in the GREEN (reserve) LINE from DELSAUX FARM and the BAPAUME-CAMBRAI Road. Ropes the Mortars were attached to three ablers in addition to three ablers in possession. Two cold guns was supplied with 45 rounds.	
	24	11 a.m.	Enemy attacked right flank of the Brigade at DELSAUX FARM and captured the first line. No 1 gun fired some rounds at the advancing enemy and when the N.C.O. in charge discovered the enemy breaking a melee etch and the men fell back with the infantry. No 2 gun fired 25 rounds at the advancing enemy when the N.C.O. in charge moved the gun-crew & along with his own free land	

WAR DIARY
or
INTELLIGENCE SUMMARY.

Army Form C. 2118.

(Erase heading not required.)

Instructions regarding War Diaries and Intelligence Summaries are contained in F. S. Regs., Part II. and the Staff Manual respectively. Title pages will be prepared in manuscript.

Place	Date	Hour	Summary of Events and Information	Remarks and references to Appendices
	MARCH 24		With the Infantry. He reported to the nearest Infantry Officer (Capt MUNDY) and the two them pushed on in front as the enemy attack. Alternative with a Officer advance. On arrival at his gun position he found the curtain and 5 tanks intact and he immediately replaced the low cap and fired his remaining rounds at the believed enemy Headquarters. Having no more ammunition he brought his gun down to Battery Headquarters.	
		11am	Orders received that in the event of a withdrawal from the GREEN LINE being necessary Brigade should fall back to a line about 600 yards in front of BAPAUME facing due EAST. Battery Commanders arranged with Brigade Commander that he should be allowed to withdraw just before the Infantry so as to be able to carry out the methods of which four variants in the line.	
		1.30pm	Orders received for withdrawal from GREEN LINE owing to enemy penetration on the right. Battery Commander sent orders to Officers in charge of Guns on the line to withdraw and take guns at Point X and about 500 yards EAST of BAPAUME on the BAPAUME - CAMBRAI road.	

WAR DIARY
or
INTELLIGENCE SUMMARY

Army Form C. 2118.

(Erase heading not required.)

Place	Date	Hour	Summary of Events and Information	Remarks and references to Appendices
			Before these others reached the separate Officers the line had commenced to withdraw, so having fired their rounds much of the cartels were destroyed by bombs. It having been found impossible to carry them out of the four Mortars was carried out of the line the teams fell back with the Infantry fighting as such.	
BAPAUME		4 P.M.	Battery assembled at Farmyard near BAPAUME with 400 guns. Casualties to this time 16 Officers 20 O.R. Missing.	
		6.0 P.M.	Many of the mortars were so ammunition for them Battery Commander reported to C.O. 9 Cheshire Regiment and placed himself and his Battery at his disposal as Infantry. Strength 2 Officers 19 O.R.	
		11 P.M.	Battery Commander ordered by the O.C. 36 Infantry Brigade to report to Brigade Headquarters to assist Staff owing to Major having become a casualty.	
GRÉVILLERS	25	9 A.M.	Remaining Battery Officer wounded. The two Mortars had to be abandoned as the fighting so near the line at the 13 O.R. of the Battery became merged in the 9 CHESHIRE REGT and retired fighting with them through IRLES DUISIEUX to MARTINPUICH.	

Army Form C. 2118.

WAR DIARY
or
INTELLIGENCE SUMMARY.
(Erase heading not required.)

Place	Date	Hour	Summary of Events and Information	Remarks and references to Appendices
HENU	28	7 a.m.	13 O.R of the Battery reported by Brigade orders to 252th Command? R.A. Battery at Brigade transport lines at HENU	
	29	2 p.m.	Battery proceeded by March route to billets in FAMECHON	
FAMECHON	29	5.30 a.m.	Battery left billets and proceeded by March route to CANDAS and entrained there at 12 Noon for the 2nd Army area. Arrived at CAËSTRE at 10 P.M. and proceeded by Motor Lorry to FUSILIER CAMP near KEMMEL arriving at 1 a.m.	
KEMMEL	30 to 31		Battery billeted in FUSILIER CAMP. 8 new mortars drawn from D.A.D.O.S. 19 Division to replace those lost in action. Strength 7 Officers 2 Officers att. 37 O.R.	

56th Brigade.

19th Division.

56th LIGHT TRENCH MORTAR BATTERY

APRIL 1918.

56th T.M. Bty.

Army Form C. 2118.

WAR DIARY
or
INTELLIGENCE SUMMARY.
(Erase heading not required.)

APRIL 1915

Place	Date	Hour	Summary of Events and Information	Remarks and references to Appendices
LINDENHOEK	1	3 pm	Battery billeted in FUSILIER CAMP. T.3.d.1.9. (Sheet 28) Proceeded by march route to RAMILLIES CAMP by order of 58th Infantry Brigade. Camp found to be occupied by Australian troops so O.C. Battery reported to Brigade Major and returned to but instructions to return to FUSILIER CAMP.	
		9 pm	Orders received from Brigade to move to APEX CAMP on arrival prior to be completed by 12 noon	
	2	10 am	Battery proceeded by march route to APEX CAMP. N.33.c.6.4 (Sheet 28)	
		7 pm	Orders received from Brigade to move to Field Punishment Camp on 3 instant	
WULVERGHEM	3	10 am	Battery proceeded by march route to Field Punishment Camp T.10 Central (Sheet 28)	
			Tramway carried out in gas war camp	
	9	4 am	A heavy bombardment opened by the enemy on Bremont front. Battery stood to and awaited orders	
	10	5 am	Owing to shelling of camp battery moved to valley T.10.a.1.9. more being reported to Brigade H.Q.	
NEUVE EGLISE		6 am	Orders received from Brigade for Battery to proceed to LA TROMPE CABT T.9.d.41. where Battery H.Q. were established	

WAR DIARY or INTELLIGENCE SUMMARY.

Army Form C. 2118.

April 1918

II

(Erase heading not required.)

Place	Date	Hour	Summary of Events and Information	Remarks and references to Appendices
NEUVE EGLISE	10	11am	O.C. 56th Infantry Brigade gave Battery Commander verbal instructions to mount 2 mortars on HILL 63 (V.13 Sheet 28) to assist in defence thereof. O.C. Battery visited O.C. 1/4 K.S.L.I. to ascertain his wishes and broke back the 2 mortars. 1/70 rounds to HILL 63.	
HILL 63.		5 pm	No 1 gun mounted at T.18 d.92 firing down southern slopes of HILL 63 and No 2 gun mounted at V.13 a.13 firing at cross roads at V.13 c.68	
	11	12 Noon	Battery H.Qrs. moved forward to Camp at T.10 d.31. Enemy attacked from PLOEGSTEERT WOOD but did not come within range. So the men were temporarily attached to 1/4 K.S.L.I. as infantry and assisted a company of that Battalion in forming a defensive flank	
		5 pm	G.O.C. 56th Infantry told Battery Commander that the mortars on HILL 63 were to remain in position unless 1/4 K.S.L.I. were forced to withdraw, in which case they would inflict as many casualties on the enemy as possible and withdraw with the infantry	
		5:30 pm	Battery Commander gave orders to this effect to Lieut Walker and ordered him to bring back 1 the mortars if possible and if not possible to destroy them	

Army Form C. 2118.

WAR DIARY
or
INTELLIGENCE SUMMARY.

(Erase heading not required.)

April 1918.

Instructions regarding War Diaries and Intelligence Summaries are contained in F. S. Regs., Part II. and the Staff Manual respectively. Title pages will be prepared in manuscript.

Place	Date	Hour	Summary of Events and Information	Remarks and references to Appendices
HILL 63	11	7pm	Enemy attacked HILL 63. The mortars were fired point blank into the advancing waves and inflicted many casualties when the 70 rounds had been fired the guns (withdrew) carrying the guns & proceeded to camp near DRANOUTRE at S.7.35.B.0.8. (Sheet 28)	
		9.30pm	Battery HQrs established at Brigade HQ rs from at S.12.a.0.8. (Sheet 28)	
		11.30pm	Battery left farm and proceeded by march route to camp at S.7.35.B.0.8.	
DRANOUTRE	12	2am	HQrs established in camp at S.7.35.B.0.8.	
		6am	Sent orders and teams from HILL 63 (reported) to O.C. Battery at camp.	
		8.45pm	Battery proceeded by march route to farm at R.18.a.6.9. (Sheet 27) in WESTOUTRE - BERTHEN Road.	
WESTOUTRE		11pm	HQrs established in this farm.	
	13	12 Noon	Orders received from Brigade to move at 2pm to KEPPEL SHELTERS N.19.d (Sheet 28)	
		2pm	Left farm and proceeded by march route to KEPPEL SHELTERS. On arrival the Enemy was found to be shelling the camp so Battery billeted in farm at N.19.d.33	
KEPPEL		5pm	Sent orders to report to 9th Cheshire Regt. for temporary attachment.	
		5.30pm	Battery billeted with Brigade HQ rs at BUTTERFLY FARM N.19.a.6.9.	

Army Form C. 2118.

WAR DIARY April 1918
INTELLIGENCE SUMMARY

(Erase heading not required.)

IV

Place	Date	Hour	Summary of Events and Information	Remarks and references to Appendices
KEMMEL	16	2pm	G.O.C. 56th Infantry Brigade instructs O.C. Battery to attach 1/7 Ottrs. to 1/4 K.S.L.I. as Infantry	
SCHERPENBERG		2.30pm	Battery moves with Brigade H.Qrs to the SCHERPENBERG.	
		10pm	Brigade Commander instructs O.C. Battery to place two mortars in positions of defense on KEMMEL HILL. O.C. Battery took 2 guns and 80 rounds there and the guns were dug in.	
	17	2.30am	Guns in position, each supplied with 40 rounds.	
			No 1 Gun at N.26.b.68 firing at LINDENHOEK. No 2 Gun at N.26.d.89 firing towards KEMMEL Church.	
		8am	O.Ps. withdrawn from 1/4 K.S.L.I. to Battery H.Qrs. Division relieved by a French Division. Battery marches to camp at L.23.c.1.2 (Sheet 27) where 11 m.o. Batteries with 56th Infantry Brigade H.Qrs. The mortars on KEMMEL HILL were brought out & carried by their teams to this camp	
WIPPENHOEK	20	11.50pm	Orders received from Brigade for move to TUNNELLERS CAMP F.27.a (Sheet 27) on 21st inst.	
	21	7.25am	Battery proceeded to march with Brigade to TUNNELLERS CAMP, arriving at 11.10am	
ST JAN-TER BIEZEN	to 25		Training carried out in fields near camp	
		1.30pm	Orders received to be ready to move at short notice	
		7.50pm	Orders received to prepare to move to RENINGHELST area	
		9.30pm	O.C. Battery instructed to report to Brigade H.Qrs where details verbal instructions were given for move to RENINGHELST area	

WAR DIARY or INTELLIGENCE SUMMARY.

Army Form C. 2118.

April 1918.

Place	Date	Hour	Summary of Events and Information	Remarks and references to Appendices
	25	10.5 pm	O.C. Battery instructed to report to Brigade HQrs. Orders for move to RENINGHELST area (cancelled) and verbal orders given for move to BUSSEBOOM & later over billets vacated by 14th the Brigade.	
		11.40 pm	Proceeded to march route to BUSSEBOOM. Thence to OUDERDOM.	
OUDERDOM	26	3.30 am	Battery billeted in OUDERDOM with remainder of Brigade.	
		3.40 am	O.C. Battery instructed to report to Brigade HQrs in OUDERDOM. O's C. Battalions were present and Brigade issued orders as to lines to be occupied by them. Battery to be in Brigade reserve with 8th K.N. Staff. Regt.	
		2.40 pm	Battery moved to form at G.23.d.9'. (Sheet 28)	
		3.10 pm	Orders received to be ready to move at short notice.	
		6 pm	Informed by G.O.C. 56th Infantry Brigade that Brigade was attached to 49th Division.	
	28	7 pm	Orders received to be ready to move at 10 minutes notice.	
	30	3.30 pm	Warning Order received that XIX th Division would relieve XXI st Division in line from southern edge of RIDGE WOOD to FRENCH FARM 127.a.85. (Sheet 28). 58th Brigade taking over tonight, but not anticipated that 56 th Brigade would move until tomorrow.	

J. Hirst Capt
O.C. 56 T.M.Bty.

Army Form C. 2118.

WAR DIARY
or
INTELLIGENCE SUMMARY.   APRIL 1915
(Erase heading not required.)

Instructions regarding War Diaries and Intelligence Summaries are contained in F. S. Regs., Part II. and the Staff Manual respectively. Title pages will be prepared in manuscript.

Place	Date	Hour	Summary of Events and Information	Remarks and references to Appendices
LINDENHOEK	1		Battery billeted in FUSILIER CAMP. T.3.d.1.9. (Sheet 28)	
		3pm	Proceeded by march south to RAMILLES CAMP. by order of G.O.C. Infantry Brigade. (camp found) to be occupied by Australian troops. O.C. Battery reported to Brigade Major and received verbal instructions to return to FUSILIER CAMP.	
		9pm	Orders received from Brigade to move to APEX CAMP on divisional Order to be completed by 12 noon.	
	2	10 am	Battery proceeded by march route to APEX CAMP. N.33.c.6.9. (Sheet 28)	
		7 pm	Orders received from Brigade to move to Field Punishment Camp on Veltonet.	
WULVERGHEM	3 to 9	10 am	Battery proceeded by march route to Field Punishment Camp. T.10. Central. (Sheet 28) Tramway carries out in field near camp.	
	10	4 am	A heavy bombardment opened by the enemy on Wulverghem front. Battery stood to arms awaited orders.	
		5 am	Owing to shelling of camp Battery moved to valley T.10.a.19. next they reported to Brigade H.Q.	
NEUVE EGLISE	11	8 am	Orders received from Brigade for Battery (1 piece) to LA TROUPE CAMP. T.9.d.4.1. where Battery was established.	

Army Form C. 2118.

WAR DIARY
or
INTELLIGENCE SUMMARY.   April 1918
(Erase heading not required.)

Place	Date	Hour	Summary of Events and Information	Remarks and references to Appendices
NEUVE EGLISE	10	10am	O.C. 50th Infantry Brigade gave Battery Commander verbal instructions to mount 2 mortars on HILL 63 (V.13. Sheet 28) to assist in defence thereof. O.C. Battery visited O.C. 1/4 K.S.L.I. to ascertain his wishes. Find under that the 2 mortars & 70 rounds to HILL 63.	
		5pm	Nos 1 & 2 guns mounted at T.14.b.92 from battery dump of HILL 63 in N13.c.5.5 from mortars at V.13.a.1.3 from and emplaced at N.13.a.5.5.8	
HILL 63	11	12 Noon	Battery Htrs. moved forward to camp at T.14.d.31. Enemy attacks from PLOEGSTEERT WOOD did not come within range of the new guns. Temporarily attached to 1/4 K.S.L.I. as infantry and assisted a party of that Battalion in forming a defensive flank.	
		5pm	O.C. 50th Infantry Brigade told Battery Commander that the mortars on HILL 63 were to remain in position unless 1/4 K.S.L.I. were forced to withdraw, in which case they would inflict as many casualties on the enemy as possible and withdraw with the infantry.	
		5.30pm	Battery Commander gave orders to this effect to Lieut Willis and ordered him to bring back the mortars if possible and if unable to destroy them.	

Army Form C. 2118.

WAR DIARY April 1918

or

INTELLIGENCE SUMMARY.

(Erase heading not required.)

Place	Date	Hour	Summary of Events and Information	Remarks and references to Appendices
HILL 63	11	7 pm	Enemy attacked HILL 63. The Battery were firing front flank into the intervening ground and infantry many casualties when the 70 yards line fire from the Huns machine guns carrying the guns forward to camp near DRANOUTRE at H.33.C.0.8. (Sheet 28).	
		9.30 pm	Battery HQrs established at B-gade HQrs at B12a08 (Sheet 28)	
		11.30 pm	Battery left farm and proceeded by march route to camp at H35 C08	
DRANOUTRE	12	2 am	HQrs established in camp at H35 C08	
		6 am	Shell holes and fumes from HILL 63 reported to O.C. Battery at camp.	
		8.30 pm	Battery proceeded by march route to fire at N.R.H.a.6.9 (Sheet 27) in WESTOUTRE — BERTHEN Rd.	
WESTOUTRE		11 pm	HQrs established in this farm.	
	13	12 Noon	Orders received from Brigade to move at 2 pm to KEPPEL SHELTERS N17.d (Sheet 23)	
		2 pm	Left farm and proceeded by march route to KEPPEL SHELTERS in school rd.	
			Enemy was firing to Westoutre. The camp B.64th Batt'n in from N.M.G. 1.2.3	
KEPPEL		5 pm	Sent orders on & write a report to O.C. Cheshire Regt for temporary attachment.	
		5.30 pm	Battery billeted with Brigade HQrs at BUTTERFLY FARM N19.a.79	

Army Form C. 2118.

WAR DIARY
or
INTELLIGENCE SUMMARY.
(Erase heading not required.)

IV

April 1918

Place	Date	Hour	Summary of Events and Information	Remarks and references to Appendices
KEMMEL	16	2 pm	G.O.C. 50th Infantry Brigade instructed O.C. Battery to attach 1 gun to 1/4 K.S.L.I. as Infantry.	
SCHERPENBERG		2.30 pm	Battery moves with Brigade H.Q.s to Mt. SCHERPENBERG.	
			Brigade Commander instructed O.C. Battery to plant his mortars in positions of defence on KEMMEL HILL. O.C. Battery took 2 guns and 80 rounds there and the guns were dug in.	
	17	2.30 am	Guns in position, each supplemented with 40 rounds.	
			No.1 gun at N26.b.89 firing at LINDENHOEK. No 2 gun at N26.b.89 firing towards KEMMEL Church.	
		6 am	17 O.Rs. withdrawn from 1/4 K.S.L.I. to Battery Hdqrs.	
			Division relieved by a French Division. Battery marched to camp at L.23.C.12 (Sheet 27)	
WIPPENHOEK	19		When it was Attached with 50th Infantry Brigade Hdqrs. The positions on KEMMEL HILL were brought out and received by these Hdqrs. to this camp.	
	20	11.50 pm	Orders received from Brigade for move to TUNNELLERS CAMP. F.17.a (Sheet 27) at 11.10 am.	
	21	7.30 am	Battery proceeded & march out to TUNNELLERS CAMP arriving at 11.10 am.	
St JAN-Ter-BIEZEN	40 25	1.30 pm	Training carried on in form near Camp. Orders received to be ready to march Pack Shell outfit. Orders received to proceed to march to RENINGHELST a.a.	
		7.30 pm	O.C. Battery instructed to report to Brigade Hdqrs where detailed verbal instructions were given.	
		9.30 pm	1/4 March to RENINGHELST a.a.	

Army Form C. 2118.

WAR DIARY
or
INTELLIGENCE SUMMARY.
(Erase heading not required.)

Instructions regarding War Diaries and Intelligence Summaries are contained in F. S. Regs., Part II. and the Staff Manual respectively. Title pages will be prepared in manuscript.

Place	Date	Hour	Summary of Events and Information	Remarks and references to Appendices
OUDERDOM				

5th T.M. Bty

Army Form C. 2118.

WAR DIARY
or
INTELLIGENCE SUMMARY.
(Erase heading not required.)

May 1918

Place	Date	Hour	Summary of Events and Information	Remarks and references to Appendices
BURDERDICQ	1st	11.45am	Orders received for Battery to move at 12 R H.Grs to receive instructions from Bde Commander who informed them that they would proceed to the line that evening, the Lieutenant's of the 1st NOORMEZEELE – KRUISSTRAATHOEK ROAD, right south end of RIDGE WOOD. Battery was ordered to put four guns in the line to meet possible approaches.	
		2.45pm	LIEUT. ARCHER left Bdg. H.Grs to reconnoitre the line	
		4.15pm	O.C. 13 Battery called on the Bde Commander and received permission to put two guns in position tonight and the remaining two tomorrow night, owing to the small number of ammunition for the carrying party	
		6.0pm	66 Infty Bde under B.M.G. 68° containing instructions in relief received	
		7.45pm	Battery proceeded by March Route to RIDGE WOOD. Arrived two guns and 80 bombs and picked up and carried with them 1 gun N9a6 (SHEET 28) and M.O. of guns started with wood. Not own were laid on tops opposite H.M.5.7.24 and No 2 gun in BRASSERIE – RIDGE WOOD ROAD.	
DICKEBUSCH	2nd	1.25am	Battery H.Grs established with 196 H.Grs at H.27.b.78.	
		10.30am	O.C. Battery visited 3 Battalion H.Grs and the mortars in RIDGE WOOD and arrangements O.C.I/4 R.S.L.I that officer in charge of the guns in the wood should live at his H.Grs.	
		9.0am	20 bombs taken to the guns in RIDGE WOOD making 50 per gun.	
		11.0pm	Battery left H.Grs with O.C. and proceeded to (CAFÉ BELGE and from there carried 2 mortars and 30 bombs, via SCOTTISH WOOD to ELZENWALLE	
	3rd	1.15am	2 guns in position at H.36 a.8.2 (Sheet 28) near ELZENWALLE. The 3 gun laid on road at H.36.d.4.2. and No.4 gun on road at H.36.6.9.3. Each gun supplied with 15 bombs.	
		10.0am	500 bullets rings received from Divn. H.Grs	
		11.0am	O.C. Battery visited three Battalion H.Qrs, two advanced Battery H.Grs and guns in the line	
ZILLEBEKE		3.30pm	57 Infty Bde B.M. 1694 received giving warning of probable enemy attack from tomorrow. M.E.P.R.15	
		6.20pm	Heavy artillery fire opened by the enemy on Dickebusch front opposite the front of the 19 Divisional front. Bombarded on to 1st target S.O.S. sent up on the right but outside XIX Divisional front.	

Army Form C. 2118.

WAR DIARY
or
INTELLIGENCE SUMMARY.
(Erase heading not required.)

May-1917

Instructions regarding War Diaries and Intelligence Summaries are contained in F.S. Regs., Part II. and the Staff Manual respectively. Title pages will be prepared in manuscript.

Place	Date	Hour	Summary of Events and Information	Remarks and references to Appendices
DICKEBUSCH	3rd	8.30pm	No 1 Stokes Mortar in RIDGE WOOD fired 25 rounds into enemy ground at N5.d.2.4.	
		10.0pm	Twenty rounds and 6 guns 3 and 4 at ELZENWALLE making 50 rounds in gun.	
	4th	12.30am	Message received from 58 Inf Bde's front concerning to fire at enemy attack in morning.	
		1.0am	Officer & 6 guns 3.4 moved by order of O.C. Battery & support 6 guns at ELZENWALLE CHATEAU	
		4.20am	Enemy had stronly preformed front and S.W. north through the SOS signal was up.	
			Divisional Front. Gun emplacement in RIDGE WOOD was thoroughly ended.	
		10.20am	O.C. Battery visited 13th London Division.	
		2.30pm	Warning order received from 98 Infantry Brigade and gun in the morning	
			98 Infantry Brigade to relieve 13 Infantry Brigade that Brigade was to relieved by	
		4.20pm	98 Infantry Brigade. B.M.G 114 receiving continuing orders for a lift.	
		4.30pm	2nd in Command of 98 & 4 inch mortar Battery arrived and made arrangements for	
			relief.	
	5th	9.55pm	98 4 inch Mortar Battery arrived at Battery HQrs, guides took relieving team to the line	
		2.30am	Relief complete. B Stokes marched 6 camp at G.21.b.3.8 (SHEET 28) and arrived there at 7am.	
		11.50am	Warning order received from Bde for Bn in same to area west of POPERINGHE this afternoon.	
		1.0am	57 Infantry Brigade operation order No 126 received.	
		3.0pm	Battery proceeded by March Route to L.14.b.3.3 (SHEET 27) and camped then.	
ST.JAN.TER- BIEZEN	6th	5.0pm	Battery moved from x L 7.a.9.6 (SHEET 27)	
	7th	9.0am	Warning received that as aids of Brigade are to be ready to move at half an hours notice.	
		12 noon	Warning order received that Brigade would return 58th Brigade in the line in the spring	
	8th	8.20am	Warning received from Brigade & be ready to move at 10 mins notice.	
		9.0am	Warning cancelled	
	9th	9.30pm	Warning that received that Brigade would relieve 58 Infantry Brigade in the line on the 10th to 11th.	
	10th	7.20am	58 Infantry Brigade Operation Order No 125 received	
		5.30pm	Battery Kennels and proceeded by march route to HOPOUTRE SIDING gear Pop at N.9.H.S. arrived at 7.30pm and proceeded through the line	

Army Form C. 2118.

Instructions regarding War Diaries and Intelligence Summaries are contained in F. S. Regs., Part II and the Staff Manual respectively. Title pages will be prepared in manuscript.

WAR DIARY
or
INTELLIGENCE SUMMARY.

May 1918

(Erase heading not required.)

Place	Date	Hour	Summary of Events and Information	Remarks and references to Appendices
	13th	9.10 pm	Received information that relief of Bgn by 172 MTMBY in pgns at L.22 A.9.1 near CAFE BELGE from own mortars takes place four hours in the time.	
			Relief completed	
	14th	3.30 am		
		11.0 am	O.C. 21st TMBy arrived at Battery H.qrs. to complete arrangements for relief tomorrow evening	
		4.30 pm	O.C. Battery visited Battalion Commanders and guns in the line	
		8.30 pm	200 rounds taken up to the mortars and distributed so as to leave 100 bombs with each gun.	
		8.53 pm	S.O. Fifty Field Operation Order No. 126 received with instructions for the relief	
		10.10 pm	Message received from Bde. stating that local enemy attack is to be expected in the morning	
	12th	12.10 am	Further warning of expected attack received	
		3.10 am	Continued artillery fire directed against enemy assembly positions until 5.0 am.	
		1.0 pm	O.C. Battery visited guns and Battalion Commanders	
		6.40 pm	21st TMBy arrived at Battery H.qrs.	
		8.20 pm	Teams of 21st TMBy gun were with guides to take over in the line	
		9.0 pm	Battery Hdqrs. heavily shelled until 9.40 pm April 200 4.2 & 5.9 shells were direct.	
		10.30 pm	against the farm buildings and 3 direct hits were obtained	
			Relief complete. Battery proceeded by march route and 60 cm railway to Farm L.70.96 (SHEET 2) near ST-JAN-TER-BIEZEN. arriving at 2.10 am on the 13th inst.	
ST-JAN-TER-	14th	12.30 pm	Administrative instructions 7.10 for march route by rail received from IXth Corps	
BIEZEN	16th	2.30 pm	Battery proceeded by March Route to WINNEZEELE and proceeded via DUNKERQUE - CALAIS - BOULOGNE - NOYELLES -	
	17th	12.45 am	Train left WAVELENBURG EU - ABBANCOURT - PONTOISE - CHATEAU THIERRY - CHALONS - SUR-MARNE to VITRY-LA-VILLE	
VITRY-LA-VILLE	18th	3.10 pm	Train arrived at VITRY-LA-VILLE. Battery marched & billets in LA-CHAUSSEE-SUR-MARNE	
LA CHAUSSEE-	19th		Day spent in cleaning up.	
SUR-MARNE.	20th to 26th		Systematic Training carried out by the Battery in the Stokes Gun and in ordinary Infantry work	
	27th	11 am	4 pr French Trench Mortars sent to the Battery with a supply of bombs. French spend Mortar fired	

Army Form C. 2118.

WAR DIARY
or
INTELLIGENCE SUMMARY.

(Erase heading not required.)

May 1918

Instructions regarding War Diaries and Intelligence Summaries are contained in F. S. Regs., Part II. and the Staff Manual respectively. Title pages will be prepared in manuscript.

Place	Date	Hour	Summary of Events and Information	Remarks and references to Appendices
LA CAUCEE SUR MARNE	27th	10 p.m.	Warning received from Brigade that Brigade is likely to move at short notice.	
	28th	7.3 a.m.	No. 56 Infantry Brigade Operation Order No. 126 received with instructions for move. Transport this day to area JUVIGNY – TOURS and for subsequent move Transport to LA VILLEN- TARDINOIS S.S.W. of RHEIMS. Warning given that personnel would move by bus at a date to be notified later.	
		9.0 a.m.	Advanced billeting party of 1 Officer and 1 O.R. left to proceed to new area.	
		9.15 a.m.	Battery turned out and proceeded to training area by roads.	
		10.30 a.m.	Battery transport left and joined remainder of Brigade transport at ONEY.	
		6.10 p.m.	Orders received from Brigade that Battery would not go into action but would remain in present billets, and Brigade transport of Battery would remain with Brigade.	
		6.20 p.m.	Orders received from Brigade Transport O.C. Battery he would be engaged probably up to 9 pm training with Brigade. Battery to be ready to move any time after 9.30 pm.	
		9.35 p.m.	Orders received from Brigade that Battery would move tonight.	
		9.30 p.m.	Orders received direct from Brig. H.Q. Battery to report forthwith and proceed to a destination to be indicated. M Officer who would from Brigade.	
		10.35 p.m.	Confirmation of this order received with instructions to move with all guns & Lorries arrived.	
	29th	12.35 a.m.	Battery set off on Lorries.	
		1.15 a.m.	Battery settled in CHAMBRECY 17 kilos S.W. of RHEIMS.	
		11.10 a.m.	56 Infantry Brigade B.M. 1668 received stating that a gap so reported on the line between BROUILLET and that S.7 & S.8 1st Brigade had not got forward with other FAVEROLLES and BROUILLET. 56 Infantry remaining in CHAMBRECY w. personnel reserve to be established. The situation SE is regular.	
CHAMBRECY POURCY	30th	12.30 p.m.	Staff Captain 56 Infty Brigade instructed OC Battery to march Battery and part of Bus HQ on to CHAUMUZY and establish a rear Bde Hd Qrs there and billet the Battery. On the way there orders were changed and Battery was told to proceed to Transport lines of the Brigade in field near the Mill ½ mile South of the MARFAUX – POURCY Road. Battery arrived at field at 5.30 p.m.	

Army Form C. 2118.

WAR DIARY
or
INTELLIGENCE SUMMARY.
(Erase heading not required.)

Instructions regarding War Diaries and Intelligence Summaries are contained in F. S. Regs., Part II. and the Staff Manual respectively. Title pages will be prepared in manuscript.

May 1918

Place	Date	Hour	Summary of Events and Information	Remarks and references to Appendices
POURCY	31st	6.50am	Orders received for Battery to move with 130th Hd Gr and transport of 45 Brigade to field on Eastern side of NANTEVIL-HAUTVILLERS Road at junction of that Road and Road leading to FLEURY	
NANTEUIL LA FOSSE		8.54am	Battery paraded and marched off, arriving at new camp at 11 a.m.	
		10.35pm	Orders received from Brigade for Battery to proceed to the line as Infantry to reinforce 91 Cheshire Regt	
		11.10pm	Battery moved off and marched to CHAUMUZY where O.C. Battery reported at 13th Bde H.Q rs for instructions. Received orders to occupy front of reserve line running from BOIS d'ECLISSE to BOIS de RHEIMS astride the CHAUMUZY - SARCY Road.	

J.Howie Capt
OC. 56 T.M. B14

WAR DIARY
or
INTELLIGENCE SUMMARY.

Army Form C. 2118. **Duplicate**

May 1918

Place	Date	Hour	Summary of Events and Information	Remarks and references to Appendices
BUDENDEM	1st	11.45am	Orders received for OC Battery to call at Bde HQrs to receive instructions from Bde Commander. Intelligence report that guns were registering on KRUISSTRAAT ROAD – KROISTRAATEN ROAD – as it afforded enemy RIDGE WOOD Battery was moved to new position as the first to avoid enemy approaches.	
		2.45pm	LIEUT. ARCHER LEFT BATTERY HQrs TO RETURN TO THE LINE	
		11.45pm	O.C. Battery attended Bde. Conference and received permission to fire too gun on position occupied by the enemy in the surround, owing to the small number of shells available for every gun.	
		6.0pm	S.O.S Rifle orders B.M.G. S.O.S. continuing instructions	
		7.45pm	Battery proceeded up through North of CAFE BELGE. In every round fired the battery shifted and scored to RIDGE WOOD. 50 rounds of H.E. No.a 6.4 (SHEETS) and 20 Rapide. Located with each gun. Hot gun was laid on the ground at N.45.124 and fire a burst on BRASSERIE – RIDGE WOOD ROAD.	
DICKEBUSCH	2nd	1.30am	Battery all guns established with HQrs at H.24.6.15	
		10.10am	OC Battery visited 3 Battalion HQrs and the mortars in RIDGE WOOD, and arranged with OC 2th N.S.L.I. and officers in charge of the guns as the nearest line at the HQr.	
		7.0pm	30 bombs fired at the guns in RIDGE WOOD firing 50/bag.	
		9.0pm	Battery Left HQrs under O.C. and moved to CAFE BELGE and from there crossed 2 barrage and 30 bombs on SCOTTISH ROAD E. ELZENWALLE	
	3rd	1.45am	2 guns in position at H.36 & E.1 (SHEET 28) near ELZENWALLE H.3.9.n. laid on road at H.36.d.4.2. and Moss guns in road at H.36.h.3. Each gun supplied with 15 bombs.	
		10.6am	500 Intestills rounds received from Rep. H.6°.	
		11.0am	O.C. Battery made three Battalion HQrs. two advanced Battery H.Qr. and gave H.Qr. in the Line.	
		3.30pm	57 Lightface B.M. 1494 received giving meaning of suitable enemy attack from ZILLEBEKE – MERRIS tomorrow	
		8.25pm	Heavy artillery fire opened by the enemy on Divisional front and on the front of the Brigade in the night. S.O.S. sent up on the right by north XIX Divisional group

WAR DIARY or INTELLIGENCE SUMMARY

Army Form C. 2118.

May 1918

Place	Date	Hour	Summary of Events and Information	Remarks and references to Appendices
DICKEBUSCH	3rd	5.30pm	No. 1 Notice Board at RIDGEWOOD for 4.25 rounds 114 (one group) at N.5.1.24.	
		11.0pm	Hostile barrels sent to gun zone at the ELZENWALLE pushing 50 rounds per gun.	
	4th	12.30pm	Message received from 56 Bgde SAA wrong component, suitable arrived 7.45am on return	
		1.0am	Officer of Gun No. 3 + 4 moved by orders of OC Battery to engage at ELZENWALLE (SHEET 29)	
		4.30am	Officer and Gunner of Divisional Trench Mortar Batty take up post through the SOS support and open	
			Divisional Trench Mortar emplacements in BUGY Wood used for firing signals	
		10.10am	OC Battery order received from 57 Infantry Brigade Commander arranged new firing on this position	
		2.30pm	Warning order received from 57 Infantry Brigade that Brigade would be relieved by	
			98 Infantry Brigade To night	
		4.30pm	56 Infantry Brigade BMG 114 received continuing orders for relief	
			2nd Lieut Cornwall of 9.80 trench mortar battery arrived and made arrangements for	
			relief	
	5th	9.30pm	98 Infantry Brigade Battery relief arrived battery HQ + guns took over relieving them to the line	
		2.30am	Relief complete. Battery received 6 lamps at G.2.1.B.36. (SHEET 28) and number them as 2 + 3.	
		11.30am	Wiring party received from Bgde for one to lay end of PEPERINGHE tin gas	
		1.05pm	36 Infantry Bge Operation Order No. 154 received	
		3.0pm	Battery provided by wind made to L.14.6.33.(SHEET 27)and occupied there.	
ST. JAN-TER-BIEZEN	6th	5.0pm	Battery moved to farm at A.7.9.9. (SHEET 27)	
	7th	9.0am	Warning received that all unit of Brigade are to be ready to move at 48 hours notice	
	8th	12.0pm	Warning order received that Brigade would relieve 55th Brigade on the line in the 2 days	
		8.30am	Warning received from Brigade to be ready to move at 48 hours notice	
	9th	7.0am	Warning cancelled.	
		9.0pm	Warning just received that Brigade would relieve 55th Infantry Brigade in the	
			line on the 11th inst.	
	10th	7.0am	57 Infantry Brigade Operation Order No.155 received	
		3.0pm	Battery limbered and proceeded by road and rail to mop up to the SIDING near	
			POPERINGHE where to entrained at 7.30pm and proceeded forward the line	

WAR DIARY
or
INTELLIGENCE SUMMARY.

Army Form C. 2118.

(Erase heading not required.)

Place	Date	Hour	Summary of Events and Information	Remarks and references to Appendices
	10th	1.10am	Battery limbered up and proceeded to an form at L.22.A.91 near CAPE BELGE from short march took the team to the Wagon Lines on the lines	
	11th	3.00am	Whole day quiet	
		various	Hostile aircraft over battery H.Q. & engaged the accompanying our relief however our work was going on for the lot	
		8.15pm	C.O. & Major Dorrington came up for inspection & to hand over. 100 bombs & 4 rest gas & one man from Don. Battery came to us for instruction with vertical bow for the night	
	12th	10.40pm	Nothing exciting from Dth watch tho that Brit enemy attack is to be expected in the morning	
		12.30am	Continuous intermittent H.E. shelling all night	
		1.15am	Heavy gas attack followed by Tr.M. & field guns and enemy assembly positions until 3am	
		1.15pm	Nothing unusual	
		6.40pm	Finally arrived at Battery H.Qs	
		9.30pm	Teams of 71st March Bde left with guides & take over the lines	
			Battery H.Qr Personell shelled with GAS from about 200 H.E. & S.G. shells were directed against the farm buildings and 3 direct hits were obtained relief complete	
ST. JAN-TER-BIEZEN	14th	10.30am	Battery marching order, proceeded by March Route and arrived at 2.10am on the 13th cont	
	16th	7.30pm	9 mins minutes instructing H.Q. to N. mode of rail moved	
	17th	12.45am	Battery purchased by March Route to WINNENBURG and entrained there at 10.30pm	
			from WINNENBURG and proceeded via DUNKERQUE—CALAIS—BOULOGNE—NOYELLES—Co—ABBEVILLE COURT—PONTHUSE—CHATEAU THIERRY—CHALONS SUR MARNE to VITRY-LA-VILLE	
VITRY-LA VILLE	18th	3.10pm	Train arrived at VITRY-LA-VILLE. Battery marched to billets in LA CHAUSSEE-SUR-MARNE	
LA CHAUSSEE SUR-MARNE	19th		Day spent in cleaning up	
	20th		Billets inspected, transport detail. Inc by the Battery on the Photo-Gun and in ordinary infantry work	
	21st			
	22nd			
	23rd			
	24th			
	27th	11am	Two french liaison Missifen came to the Battery with a supply of bombs, for use French mortars fires.	

Army Form C. 2118.

WAR DIARY
or
INTELLIGENCE SUMMARY.
(Erase heading not required.)

May 1918.

Instructions regarding War Diaries and Intelligence Summaries are contained in F. S. Regs., Part II. and the Staff Manual respectively. Title pages will be prepared in manuscript.

Place	Date	Hour	Summary of Events and Information	Remarks and references to Appendices
LA CROISIE SUR MARNE	27th	10 p.m.	Warning received from Brigade of move North.	
	28th	7 a.m.	36 Infantry Brigade Standfast Order No. 4 received with instruction for move of transport this day to area JUVIGNY-TROIS and to safeguard men employed in area VILLE EN TARDENOIS 3 SW of RHEIMS. Warning given that personnel would move if too wet a task & be notified later.	
		9 a.m.	Advanced billeting party of 1 Officer and O.R. left & proceeded to new area.	
		9:15 a.m.	Waiting to detail and proceed with horses and whole Battery.	
		10:30 a.m.	Gunners transport left and joined remainder of Brigade transport in GUEUX area.	
		6 a.m.	Orders received from Brigade the Battery would go into action, but would remain in present billets with horses harnessed up saddled.	
		8 p.m.	Orders received from Brigade that gun teams to report would be conveyed probably by lorry to report Brigade Headquarters at WALLY to meet Lorries after 9.30 p.m.	
		9.30 p.m.	Orders received from Brigade that Battery would move tonight	
		9.40 p.m.	Orders received from Brigade for Battery to meet Officer of Brigade on road in vicinity of 1 mile S. East from Bruges with instructions to a destination and to ascertain by Officer in Charge of Brigade with instructions & move with all guns baggage & transport. Information of this	
		10.30 p.m.	Baggage arrived.	
	29th	12:15 a.m.	Waiting set off in tours in CHAMBRECY 17 miles SW of RHEIMS	
		1:30 a.m.	Waiting trailer with Infantry Brigade B.M. 36th arrived stating that a gap in position on the line between FAVEROLLES and BROUILLET and that 59, 158 K of yards front & one forward with orders to reconnoitre BROUILLET and that 59, 158 K of yards in CHAMBRECY in reconnoitred Reserve	
		2 p.m.	& carried the situation. 36 13 Brigade remaining in CHAMBRECY in reconnoitred Reserve	
		2:40 p.m.		
CHAMBRECY POURCY	30th	12.30 p.m.	Staff Captain 36 Infty Brigade informed CC Battery to march Battery and part of 13th Hd Grs to CHAUMUZY and established near Bde Hd Grs there and till the Battery Hrs the way thither we were observed and Battery was told to proceed to transport lines of the Brigade in field near the Hill 2 mile South of the MARFAUX - POURCY Road. Battery arrived at field at 3.30 p.m.	

D. D. & L., London, E.C.
(A800) Wt. W17/M2031 730,000 5/17 Sch. 52 Forms/C2118/14

Army Form C. 2118.

WAR DIARY
or
INTELLIGENCE SUMMARY.

(Erase heading not required.)

May 1918

Place	Date	Hour	Summary of Events and Information	Remarks and references to Appendices
POURCY	31st	4.30am	Firing noticed on Battery. Ground was notified that G.O. and I officer of Brigade to join in eastern end of NANTEUIL-NADIVILLERS Road at junction of that road (read leading to FLEURY.	
NANTEUIL LA FOSSE		8.30am	Battery harnessed and marched off, arriving at new camp at 11am.	
		10.55pm	Orders received from Brigade for Battery to proceed to the line as Infantry to reinforce 9th (Midland) Regt.	
		11.10pm	Battery moved off and marched to CHAUMUZY where OC Battery reported at 158th Inf. Bde. for instructions. Received orders to occupy part of reserve line running from BOIS d'EILLISSE to BOIS in RHEIMS astride the CHAUMUZY-SARCY road	

Army Form C. 2118.

WAR DIARY
or
INTELLIGENCE SUMMARY. Oct 1918

(Erase heading not required.)

Instructions regarding War Diaries and Intelligence Summaries are contained in F. S. Regs., Part II. and the Staff Manual respectively. Title pages will be prepared in manuscript.

Place	Date	Hour	Summary of Events and Information	Remarks and references to Appendices
CHAMOUZY	7/10		[illegible handwritten entries]	
BOIS DE COURTON	7th	5 am		
		6 pm		
	8th	3.9 pm		
		3.15 pm		
	9th			
	10th			
	11th			
	12th	7.30 pm		
		20 —		

Army Form C. 2118.

WAR DIARY
or
INTELLIGENCE SUMMARY.
(Erase heading not required.)

Instructions regarding War Diaries and Intelligence Summaries are contained in F. S. Regs., Part II. and the Staff Manual respectively. Title pages will be prepared in manuscript.

Place	Date	Hour	Summary of Events and Information	Remarks and references to Appendices
	12th		[illegible]	
	13th			
	14th			
	15th			
	16th			
	17th		Marching orders. Provisional Relief of the [illegible] sepn Brigade was to take place in the neighb. of [illegible]	
			9th [illegible] Orders received at 2.15 pm.	
	18th		Left [illegible] [illegible] at 9 am	
			[illegible] [illegible] be relieved by the 47 Div whose guns being retained. C Battalion in Billets	
			through the day.	
	19th	3.10am	191st Bde at work clear L MARTYN = 63	
	20th	2.30am	Battery proceeded by March Route to LE MESNIL	
	21st	5.45am	9th Battery entrained & proceeded to RENNES.	
RENNES	21-29			
	30th	5.45am	Battery carried out a scheme of infantry training under the supervision of Lt Col. S.H. Stafford RFA	
			Battery paraded by march route to DROUSSY, le GRAND (staying [illegible] arrived 10.30 am.	

WAR DIARY
or
INTELLIGENCE SUMMARY. July 1918.

(Erase heading not required.)

Army Form C. 2118.

Place	Date	Hour	Summary of Events and Information	Remarks and references to Appendices
BRUAY-LE-GRAND	1st		Battery equipped at HAGING AND BRUAY-LE-GRAND.	
ROUSSEAUVILLE	2nd	2.0 a.m	Battery proceeded by March Route to FERE CHAMPENOISE & were entrained at 10.0 a.m. & proceeded by rail to MARESQUEL. Train journey about 26½ hours.	
ERGNY	4th 5th	4.30 p.m	Battery detrained at MARESQUEL and proceeded by March Route to ROUSSEAUVILLE (staging area). Battery proceeded by March Route to ERGNY.	
	5th–12th		Battery billeted at ERGNY carrying out the usual programme of progressive training 1946 pattern as G.H.Q. rules.	
	13th	10.0 a.m	Battery proceeded to VERCHOCQ (ambushing point) & were carried from there by bus to ARMETTES arriving about 2.30 p.m.	
AMMETTES	14th		Battery billeted at AMMETTES carrying out programme of training, including the firing of dummy bombs.	
	16th 10.30 p		Battery and Lieut J.F. ADDISON carried out & maintained at MOUNT BERNENCHON. Battery carried out advanced training including the firing of dummy bombs.	

Instructions regarding War Diaries and Intelligence Summaries are contained in F. S. Regs., Part II. and the Staff Manual respectively. Title pages will be prepared in manuscript.

> 56TH TRENCH MORTAR BATTERY.
> No. J.A. 829
> 3-10-18

To

56 Infantry Bde

Herewith War Diary for month of September
Please acknowledge

John Fisher Capt
O C 56 T.M.B

Army Form C. 2118.

WAR DIARY August 1918
or
INTELLIGENCE SUMMARY.

(Erase heading not required.)

Instructions regarding War Diaries and Intelligence Summaries are contained in F. S. Regs., Part II. and the Staff Manual respectively. Title pages will be prepared in manuscript.

Place	Date	Hour	Summary of Events and Information	Remarks and references to Appendices
AMETTES	1st		Inter Light Trench Mortar Battery Competition 19th Division. This Battery obtained the highest marks in Ranging, Squad Drill, and Method of carrying ammunition.	
	1st-6th		Battery carried out systematic intensive training.	
LOCON SECTOR	6th		Battery proceeded to LABEUVIERE by lorry, thence by March Route to the line relieved the Battery of the 8th Infantry Brigade - taking over 4 guns in the line (ABERDEEN LINE)	
	8th		One gun was given a roving commission in the outpost line being placed at the disposal of the Company Commander.	
	9th		On the night of the 9th this Battery co-operated with the Artillery in preparation of a raid on 2/M.G. position.	
	10th		Two other guns were subsequently placed at the disposal of the outpost Battalion & were also employed behind the outpost line on S.O.S. lines. Subsequently 2 more guns were pushed up, making in all, covering the outpost line	
			If the enemy retook the outpost line fixed forward, these guns accompanied them, being laid on fresh S.O.S. lines, according to the instructions of the outpost Battalion.	
	22-23rd		On the night of the 22nd/23rd the Battery carried out a stoop on an enemy post.	
	25th		On the 25th the guns having been laid on fresh S.O.S. lines. The guns were ranged by Lieut FJ ADDISON from an Observation Point in No-man's-land.	
	27th		On the 27th four guns were districtuted along the Line of Retention in accordance with Orders contained in a new Brigade Defence Scheme	
	28th		In the evening of the 28th this Battery was relieved by the Battery of the 57th Brigade and proceeded by March Route to the Billets at ST SAUVEUR (CHOCQUES)	
ST SAUVEUR	30-31st		Battery carried out a training programme, special attention being given to the subject of bayoneting.	

John Acher / Capt
a/c 3 T M B y

Army Form C. 2118.

Army Form C. 2118.

WAR DIARY
or
INTELLIGENCE SUMMARY.
(Erase heading not required.)

56 TMB

Place	Date	Hour	Summary of Events and Information	Remarks and references to Appendices
MIETTES	1st		[illegible] Major [illegible] complained of being [illegible] the Battery attached to the Brigade [illegible]	
LOCON SECTOR	1st-4th		had reported at [illegible] and the Battery engaging enemy trenches [illegible]	
	5th		Battery proceeded to LADEVIERE by route march to the line by march route to the line (ABERDEEN LINE) & joined the Battery of the 37th Inf Bde	
	6th		[illegible]	
	7th		[illegible] gave a heavy casualties in the [illegible] time [illegible] placed at the [illegible]	
	10th		of the Central Company. [illegible]	
			Was [illegible] that this Battery co-operated with the Battery in preparation [illegible]	
			[illegible] occupied as a Co-op position	
			On other posts was subsequently placed at the disposal of the asst Battalion & was [illegible] during the attack on the [illegible] June on SOS lines. [illegible] & new guns were made [illegible]	
			[illegible] covering the entry into [illegible]	
			[illegible] the enemy [illegible] SOS lines [illegible] & recognised them very [illegible]	
	23rd		Lost [illegible] SOS lines again. The Artillery made [illegible] of the [illegible] & on [illegible] [illegible]	
	25th		On the 23rd the guns having been lent to the 37th Bde for [illegible] firing [illegible]	
	27th		Lieut F. T. ADDISON from a [illegible] Position returned to the unit & [illegible] in accordance with	
	29th		the orders [illegible] sent up [illegible] and [illegible] the [illegible] Division	
			On the evening of the 29th. First lot [illegible] returned by the Battery of the 37th Infantry	
			& proceeded to [illegible] Brigade [illegible] north of ST SAUVEUR (CHOCQUES)	
ST SAUVEUR	30th-31st		Battery engaged in training, programme [illegible] and Trench Trips [illegible] to the output	
			of Mieges.	

John [illegible]
Lt. 57 TMB

WAR DIARY or INTELLIGENCE SUMMARY

Army Form C. 2118.

September 1918

Place	Date	Hour	Summary of Events and Information	Remarks and references to Appendices
ST SAUVEUR	1st-4th		Battery carried out a training programme, special attention being paid to ranging and rapid digging in of gun pits.	
	5th		Battery entered at ST SAUVEUR for the first and took over the fronts held by 138th & 139th (A.M.) Brigade M & 140th (A.M.) Batteries.	
			Guns were employed to in the pathroll line + th on line of Albutson. Covering approaches via RUE DE BOIS + RUE DES BERCEAUX.	
	6th		The Battery with one gun carried out a scheme under instructions of O.C. 96 N. Staffords. Right to assist a patrol of "A" Coy to establish a stronger post at DUBOIS FARM & protect the right flank in their manoeuvre. This was carried out with good effect & marched-gun though fired on the night & cal gun shew immediately dispersed each approach to the post was well established 13 rounds in all were fired.	
	6.12th		Usual line routine	
	13th		Under instructions from O.C. 9th Cheshires then a shot was carried out and patrols worked out each to TOUQUETTE FARM to give a patrol work to go out a later core of rest time for reconnaissance work with a possibility to establish a post.	

WAR DIARY or INTELLIGENCE SUMMARY

Army Form C. 2118.

September 1918

Place	Date	Hour	Summary of Events and Information	Remarks and references to Appendices
	13th		Orders to start and general the programme had to be rearranged the had time would not suffice it was deemed unwise for the Corps as the Bde's 2 platoons remained in the front and 18 rounds were lost in all.	
	15th		Under better conditions this programme was repeated and it was the best well established but are compensating with the artillery practiced in liaison. The wire entanglement established	
	16th		L.a. TOULETTE FARM, the first twenty strong-pts established. On the night of 16th–17th the battery moved up to the line of 57th Highland Light Infantry Battery who took over by first instance. The Battery after a little proceeded to Illiesville	
BAS D'ANTHEZIN	18th–19th		March to BAS D'ANTHEZIN. Programme of training carried out.	
BOIRY	20th		The Battery with 2 raised munitions at scene established the Boiry was under orders of 2nd Cheshire Bgde positions west taken up & occupied. Bn all to useful to (the) west sides are in rear 466 firing reported on strong points available by which 9 pds flat backed support after hays with North Lancs Bgy commander was given to remainder gun-fire for rear in strong points reduced.	

Army Form C. 2118.

WAR DIARY
or
INTELLIGENCE SUMMARY.
(Erase heading not required.)

September 1918

Place	Date	Hour	Summary of Events and Information	Remarks and references to Appendices
BONY	20th		This proved very successful and gave confidence to the advancing infantry.	
	22nd		The Battery relieved 58th Australian French Mortar Battery in the line on the night of 22nd/23rd moving by Motor Bus to positions in the line from Nurlu. Batteries as follows. L Battery had 3 sets of alternative positions prepared.	
	24th-28th		Line routine & necessary movement of guns for vulnerable targets were carried out under instructions of Battery Commander.	
	29th		A series of their Battery carried out a short under instruction of Bgth Battle of [???] on suspected enemy Machine Gun emplacements during a forward reconnaissance. The programme was carried out & the suspected area neutralised with good effect. 35 rounds in all were fired.	

John Foster
OC 336 Army

56 F.H. Battery

Army Form C. 2118.

WAR DIARY
or
INTELLIGENCE SUMMARY for October 1918

(Erase heading not required.)

Instructions regarding War Diaries and Intelligence Summaries are contained in F. S. Regs., Part II. and the Staff Manual respectively. Title pages will be prepared in manuscript.

Place	Date	Hour	Summary of Events and Information	Remarks and references to Appendices
	1st		Battery in the line. Left 2 guns were pushed up sents close support at	
LA MOTTE FARM				
	2nd		Enemy found to have evacuated the AUBERS RIDGE. Two guns with 30 rounds of ammunition, in charge of Lt ADDISON accompanied the support Company of 8th N. Stafford Regt and were established in AUBERS village. Battery relieved on the line by Battery of the 17th Division Battery proceeding to RAIMBERT by lorry.	
RAIMBERT	3rd			
	4th		Battery entrained at CALONNE RICOUART and proceeded to SAULTY.	
SAULTY	5.6th		Training	
	7th		Moved by motor lorry to GRAINCOURT.	
	8th		Moved to another camp West of GRAINCOURT.	
GRAINCOURT	9th		Training	
	10th		Battery proceeded by march route to PROVILLE south west of CAMBRAI	
	12th		Moved by march route to Billets in Rue Buckley CAMBRAI	

Army Form C. 2118.

WAR DIARY
or
INTELLIGENCE SUMMARY. for October 1918
(Erase heading not required.)

Instructions regarding War Diaries and Intelligence Summaries are contained in F. S. Regs., Part II. and the Staff Manual respectively. Title pages will be prepared in manuscript.

Place	Date	Hour	Summary of Events and Information	Remarks and references to Appendices
CAMBRAI	15-16th		A systematic training in open warfare tactics carried out employing mules & limbers as transport	
	17th		March route to AVESNES where the Battery went billets	
	18th		Orders received (cancelled later) to return to ST AUBERT.	
	19th		In the evening battery moved by march route to ST AUBERT being the Brigade in close support of Divisional operations at HAUSSY.	
ST AUBERT	20th		Moved into assembly position of support during the attack on the SELLE River	
	21st		Billeted at ST AUBERT.	
	22nd		Orders received on relief of Division to proceed to CAGNONCLES.	
	23rd		Moved by march route across country to CAGNONCLES	
	24th		Returned by march route across country to ST AUBERT the Brigade being in special reserve to drawthand by the 61st Division	
	25th		Orders to return to CAGNONCLES the following day	
	26th		Returned by march route to CAGNONCLES.	
CAGNONCLES	27th		Battery in billets	

Army Form C. 2118.

WAR DIARY
or
INTELLIGENCE SUMMARY. for October 1918

(Erase heading not required.)

Instructions regarding War Diaries and Intelligence Summaries are contained in F. S. Regs., Part II. and the Staff Manual respectively. Title pages will be prepared in manuscript.

Place	Date	Hour	Summary of Events and Information	Remarks and references to Appendices
CAGNONCLES	25-31st		A system of advanced attack training was carried out by the Brigade. Each Battalion had one section of Trench Mortars attached for these operations. Limbers & mules being used to carry guns & ammunition.	

John Acker Capt
TMB

WAR DIARY or INTELLIGENCE SUMMARY

Army Form C. 2118.

for October 1918

52 TMB

Place	Date	Hour	Summary of Events and Information	Remarks and references to Appendices
	1st		Battery in the line. Left 2 guns were pushed up into close support at	
			LA MOTTE FARM	
	2nd		4 enemy found to have evacuated the AUBERS RIDGE. Two guns with 30	
			rounds of ammunition in charge of Lt ADDISON accompanied the advance	
			guard of 2/5 Bedford Regt and were established in AUBERS village	
			Battery relieved in the line by Battery of the 17th Division. Battery proceeding	
			to RAIMBERT by bus	
RAIMBERT	3rd			
	4th		Battery entrained at CABONNE RICOUART and proceeded to SAULTY	
SAULTY	5th		Training	
	7th		Moved by motor lorry to GRAINCOURT	
	8th		Moved to another camp West of GRAINCOURT	
GRAINCOURT	9th		Training	
	10th		Battery proceeded by march route to PRONVILLE south west of CAMBRAI	
	12th		March by march route to billet in RUE ROMILLY CAMBRAI	

Army Form C. 2118.

WAR DIARY
or
INTELLIGENCE SUMMARY. for October 1918
(Erase heading not required.)

Place	Date	Hour	Summary of Events and Information	Remarks and references to Appendices
CAMBRAI	16th		A systematic training in open warfare tactics carried out, supplementary works & limbers in transport.	
	17th		March route to AVESNES where the Battery was billeted	
	18th		Orders received (cancelled later) to move to ST AUBERT	
	19th		In the evening Battery moved by march route to ST AUBERT being the Brigade in close support of Divisional quarters at HAUSSY	
ST AUBERT	20th		Moved into scarcely position of support during the attack on the same from	
	21st		Billeted at ST AUBERT	
	22nd		Orders received in relief of Division & moved to CAGNONCLES	
	23rd		Moved by march route across country to CAGNONCLES	
	24th		Returned by march route across country to ST AUBERT the brigade being in general reserve to operations by the 61st Division	
	25th		Orders to return to CAGNONCLES the following day	
	26th		Returned by march route to CAGNONCLES	
CAGNONCLES	27th		Battery in billets	

WAR DIARY or INTELLIGENCE SUMMARY.

Army Form C. 2118.

for October 1915

Place	Date	Hour	Summary of Events and Information	Remarks and references to Appendices
CAGNICLES	26.30		A system of advanced attack training was carried out by the Brigade. Each Battalion had one section of French Mortars attached for these operations, smokes + smoke being used to carry guns + ammunition	

Capt
V.S.Mass.

SECRET.   W. D   COPY No. 1.

56th Infantry Brigade Operation Order No. 161.

Reference Maps 51.A. S.E. & S.W.   Dated 19-10-1918.

1. Outline of attack.

On the 20th October 19th Division will attack and capture the high ground East of the River SELLE. The Guards Division will be attacking on the right and the 4th Division on the left.

The attack will be carried out by the 57th on the right and 58th Inf. Bde. on the left.

The attack consists of two phases :-

(a)   The bridging of the River SELLE, the capture of the line of railway and the high ground in P.34.a. and d. and V.5.a., and the village of HAUSSY.

(b)   The capture of the ridge extending from MAISON BLANCHE (W.1.d.) through MAISON BLEUE to P.23.central.

2. Objectives of attack.

The objectives and boundaries of the attack will be as shown on the map already copied by representatives from Battalions.

3. Reserve Brigade.

56th Infantry Brigade will be the Reserve Brigade for the attack and will move as follows :-

(a)   On the night 19/20th October the Brigade will bivouac on the Eastern edge of ST AUBERT. This move will be carried out as follows :-

Route - U.28.b.6.4. by track to - U.29.b.0.2. - thence along Eastern side of Railway through U.29.b. and U.24.c.

Starting Point.- Railway crossing U.29.b.0.2.

Unit.	To.	Time of passing Starting Point.
8/N.Staff.R.	V.13.c.9.3.Area.	2000.
4/Shrops.L.I.	V.19.central Area.	2030.
9/Ches. R.	V.19.a.7.3.Area.	2100.
56th T.M.Bty.	V.19.a.7.6.	2115.

These bivouac areas will be as already reconnoitred. Units will notify Bde. H.Q. of the location chosen for their H.Q. by 1900 19th instant.

(b)   On the morning of 20th October probably before daybreak the Brigade will move to the high ground in V.9.central and V.15.a.0.0. and will be disposed as follows :-

4/Shrops.L.I.	round	V.15.central.
8/N.Staff.R.	round	V.9.central.
9/Ches. R.	round	V.8.d.1.1.

This move will take place when the Reserve Battalions of the leading Brigades move forward. Leading Battalions of this Brigade will each send a liaison officer to the corresponding reserve battalions of the leading brigades to report when the battalions move.

- 2 -

The move of battalions to the position in V.9. and V.15 will not take place until ordered by this Brigade.
Units will notify Bde. H.Q. of the positions selected as their H.Q. in this new position by 1900 hours 19th October.

4. **Brigade H.Q.**

Brigade H.Q. will open at V.19.a.7.6 at 2200 hours 19th inst. Further move of Bde. H.Q. will be notified to units and will be to V.20.b.6.9.

5. **Signals.**

Rifle Grenade Signals showing three Green lights and will be fired by troops on reaching the final objective.

6. **S.O.S.**

The S.O.S. Signal will be RED GREEN RED.

7. **Zero Hour.**

Zero hour will be 0200 hours 20th October. Watches will be synchronised by Brigade S.O. at 1700 hours 19th October.

8. **Hot Food.**

O.C. Units will arrange for troops to have a hot meal not later than 0400 hours 20th inst.

9. **Stragglers Posts and Prisoners Cage.**

Stragglers Posts are being established at V.19.a.9.9. and V.13.b.3.5.
Prisoners and civilians will also be taken to Stragglers Posts mentioned above.

10. During operations actual available fighting strengths of Units showing officers and other ranks separately will be sent daily to reach Brigade H.Q. at 1100 hours.

11. **1st Line Transport.**

1st Line Transport will move with Battalions to the bivouac positions. Forward of the bivouac positions pack animals will accompany battalions, the remainder of the 1st line transport will be parked under Brigade orders in ST AUBERT and will rejoin units when ordered to do so by Brigade.

12. SECRECY regarding the above operations is ESSENTIAL.
Information regarding them is to be kept back from troops in the line as long as possible, and information given to them should be the minimum compatible with the carrying out of their task.

13. ACKNOWLEDGE.

Captain,
Brigade Major,
56th Infantry Brigade.

Bde. H.Q.
GRS.

1. 9/Ches. R.
2. 4/Shrops. L.I.
3. 8/N. Staff. R.
4. 56th T.M. Bty.
5. G.O.C.
6. Bde. Major.
7. Staff Captain.
8. Bde. Signal Off.
9. War Diary (2)
10. File.
11. 19th Div. "G".
12. 57th Inf. Bde.
13. 58th Inf. Brigade.
14. D.A.P.M. 19th Div.
15. A.D.M.S. 19th Div.
16. No. 2 Coy. Div. Tr.
17. H.Q. Divl. Train.
18. Bde. Transport Off.
19. Bde. Intell: Off.
20. 19th Div. "Q".

SECRET.

56th INFANTRY BRIGADE ADMINISTRATIVE INSTRUCTIONS No.32
Issued as an Appendix to O.O.161.

1. TRANSPORT.

    A echelon will move to the Assembly positions with Battalions tonight. Such* as Battalion Commanders do not wish to keep will be sent to Brigade Transport Lines which will be established under orders of B.T.O. in U.24.a.
    B echelon will move to Bde. Transport Lines by 10 a.m. tomorrow.

2. QUARTERMASTERS' STORES.

    Q.M. stores will remain in their present locations pending receipt of further orders.

3. BLANKETS & SURPLUS KITS.

    The dump at CAMBRAI will not move at present. All blankets and packs will be dumped at billet No. 31 Rue SADI CARNOT by 8 a.m. tomorrow morning. Each unit will detail one man to act as guard who should report to the Staff Captain 6 p.m. today.

4. SURPLUS PERSONNEL.

    Surplus Personnel will be under the orders of Major J.G.MARTIN,MC.
    Men will be billetted in the large billet by the Baths.
    Officers in No.31 Rue SADI CARNOT.
    Units will send an officer of Surplus Personnel to report to Staff Captain at 6 p.m. today to be allotted accommodation for their men.

5. STRAGGLERS POSTS.

    Divisional Stragglers Posts will be established at V.19.a.9.9. and V.13.b.3.5.
    Prisoners of War will be conducted to the Stragglers Posts and handed over to representatives of the D.A.P.M.
    All released civilians will be directed to these Stragglers Posts.

6. AMMUNITION.

    Ammunition of all kinds will be delivered to any point required if the location and amount are notified to this office.

7. BURIALS.

    All units will be responsible for their own Burial arrangements. No Divisional Burial Party will be detailed. Particular is to be taken to bury all dead, both personnel and horses as soon as possible.
    No French civilians* until this office has been notified, so that a representative of the French Mission may attend.
    *will be buried

8. RETURNS.

    Units will forward to this office by 4 p.m. daily without fail
    1. CASUALTIES, giving if possible names of officers.
    2. ACTUAL BATTLE STRENGTH (Officers and other ranks) in the line.

9. WATER SUPPLY.

    Particulars of water supply in ST. AUBERT and AVESNES LEZ AUBERT were given in 19th Div. "Q" Circular No.20, forwarded to units under this office No. S.C.1796/Q. on 15.10.18.

10. **RUM.**

   Units will draw Rum from Bde. S.M. Stores today as under:-

   Each Battalion.   12 gallons.
   56th T.M.Bty.   1 gallon.

11. **MEDICAL.**

   A Car Post will be established at V.13.b.4.4. whence wounded will be taken via A.D.S. ST. AUBERT U.24.a.5.8. to M.D.S. at CAMBRAI.
   Walking wounded will proceed direct to AVESNES.
   The Car Post will be sent forward along ST. AUBERT - MONTRECOURT Road as the situation permits.

   J.T. Howe
   Captain,
   A/Staff Captain,
   56th Infantry Brigade.

Bde. H.Q.
19.10.1918.
A.J.G.

Copies to all recipients of O.O.161 plus all Quartermasters.

French Notes My
No 56 Surt 2
519 4
November 18

56
5/14

17

On His Majesty's Service.

Reference
Headquarters
19th Division

56TH TRENCH MORTAR BATTERY.
No. ST.7/0.25
Date. 2/12/17

To
  58 Infantry Bde

Would the Brigade think of
[illegible] [illegible]
[illegible] [illegible]

John Archer
Lt.
O.C. [illegible]

56th YMRBy

WAR DIARY for November 1918

INTELLIGENCE SUMMARY

Army Form C. 2118.

(Erase heading not required.)

Place	Date	Hour	Summary of Events and Information	Remarks and references to Appendices
ARTRES	1st		Battery moved by cross country route from CAGNOCLES to VENDREGIES. Battery billeted in cellars	
	2nd		Moved by march route to railway cutting behind the CHATEAU ARTRES. Here the Regtl Commander ordered two sections to be attached forthwith to the battalions about to take part in the forthcoming operations. One section under the command of Lieut. F. WHITEHEAD was attached to the 9th Cheshire Regt. The other section under the command of 2nd LIEUT. W. MYERS was attached to the 4th K.S.L.I. Each section was accompanied by Regtl pack mules for carrying supplies.	
MARESCHES	3rd		The sections remained with their respective commanders & battalions at MARESCHES	
JENLAIN	4th	06.00	The sections took part in the attack and capture of JENLAIN. Set up call was made for their services although they were well supplied with ammunition About one of the section which had been attached to the CHESHIRE Regt was transferred to the 8th N. STAFFORD Regt and took part in the attack on WARGNIES LE GRAND but again no call was made for their services. Three casualties were inflicted by the section who took 7	
WARGNIES LE GRAND			the section attached to 4th K.S.L.I. were again dispersed, accompanying their respective battalions	
WARGNIES		16.00	The Bttn was again attacked, the section accompanying their respective battalions	

Army Form C. 2118.

WAR DIARY
or
INTELLIGENCE SUMMARY. *for November 1918*

(Erase heading not required.)

Place	Date	Hour	Summary of Events and Information	Remarks and references to Appendices
TALSNIERE	10th		Orders were received to move back to BRY, which were carried out at 14:00 hrs and the	
BRY	11th		Battery was placed in rest billets.	
			At 11:00 hrs hostilities ceased, the remainder being "cease fire" rest.	
	12th		In billets at BRY.	
	13th		Orders received to proceed on the following day to VENDRIGIES.	
	14th		March by march route to rest billets at VENDRIGIES.	
	15th		March continued, the battery arrived at RIEUX about 14:00 hrs and was accommodated	
			in billets in the RUE DE LA GRAND PLACE	
RIEUX	15th-23rd		Training in steady drill etc.	
	24th		Orders received to move by march route to CAMBRAI.	
	25th		March to CAMBRAI via RAPERIE and NAVES. On arrival the battery was accommodated	
			in billets which not had previously occupied on the RUE DE RUTILLY	
CAMBRAI	26th		Battery rested	
	27th		Orders to embus were received	
	28th		09:00 The battery entrained and were conveyed by motor-bus to TALMAS via ARRAS & DOULLENS	
TALMAS	29th-30th		In rest billets at TALMAS	

John Druce Capt.
O.C. 36th Trench.

Army Form C. 2118.

WAR DIARY
or
INTELLIGENCE SUMMARY. for November 1918.
(Erase heading not required.)

Instructions regarding War Diaries and Intelligence Summaries are contained in F. S. Regs., Part II. and the Staff Manual respectively. Title pages will be prepared in manuscript.

Place	Date	Hour	Summary of Events and Information	Remarks and references to Appendices
WARGNIES-LE-	4th		Two more carriers were instructed by the section attached to 5th N. STAFFORD REGT.	
GRAND			All casualties were collected and were ammunition was sent up from Battery HG 90 which moved with Brigade HG. 90th.	
BRY	5th		The Bn. was advanced to BRY and later to FLAMENGRIE on both occasions the guns accompanied the battalion to which they were affiliated.	
FLAMENGRIE	6th		The fire was again advanced some 2000x but no call was made for the services of the affiliated guns.	
	7th	01.00	This posn. was reached on the line by the 57th Light Trench Mortars to attached and Bty. marched back to billets in ETH.	
	8th		Orders were received to proceed by march route to FLAMENGRIE but further orders were received en route that the Brigade should reach HAUDIN with all forward guns, packs and Limbers were dumped at FLAMENGRIE, and the Battery proceeded with Bgde to Gr. To HAUDIN. March immediately further orders were received to move to TAISNIERE and the Battery set out for this place by march route at 15.00 hrs	
TAISNIERE	9th		TAISNIERE was reached at 16.30 hrs and billets were found close to the Church. Rested at TAISNIERE. The personnel was relieved on the line.	

Army Form C. 2118.

WAR DIARY
or
INTELLIGENCE SUMMARY.
(Erase heading not required.)

Instructions regarding War Diaries and Intelligence Summaries are contained in F. S. Regs., Part II. and the Staff Manual respectively. Title pages will be prepared in manuscript.

Place	Date	Hour	Summary of Events and Information	Remarks and references to Appendices
ARTRES	2nd		Battn. arrived by train & motor buses from CARNIERES & VENDEGIES-[?].	
			About 7 a.m. the Bn. was ordered to march to CHATEAU ARTRES for the original [?]	
			[?] ordered two sections to be attached forthwith to the Battalions about to [?]	
			[?] part in the fothcoming operations. One section under the command of 2Lt [?]	
			2.Lt WHITEHEAD was attached to the 9th Cheshire Regt. The other section under the command of	
			2nd Lieut W. MYERS was attached to the 4th K.S.L.I. Each section was accompanied by two [?]	
			mules for carrying purposes.	
MARESHES	3rd		The sections advanced with their respective companies & battalions of MARESHES	
JENLAIN	4th	Noon	The sections took part in the attack and capture of JENLAIN where the rail was [?] & their	
			[?] though they were well supplied with ammunition.	
WARGNIES			About 1500 hrs the section which had been attached to the Cheshire Regt was transferred to	
LE GRAND			the 5th S. STAFFORD Regt. and first part in the attack on WARGNIES LE GRAND, but again no	
			call was made for their service. There casualties were sustained by this section. The guns of	
			the section attached to 4th K.S.L.I. were 4 [?] such different emplacements covering crossroads in	
			WARGNIES.	
		16:00	The Bn. was again ordered to advance the section accompanying their respective battalions.	

… Army Form C. 2118.

WAR DIARY
or
INTELLIGENCE SUMMARY. for November 1918
(Erase heading not required.)

Instructions regarding War Diaries and Intelligence Summaries are contained in F. S. Regs., Part II. and the Staff Manual respectively. Title pages will be prepared in manuscript.

Place	Date	Hour	Summary of Events and Information	Remarks and references to Appendices
WARGNIES-LE-	4th		Two more casualties were sustained by the section attached to 6th N STAFFORD REGT.	
GRAND			No casualties were received and were communicated and sent up from Battery HdQrs	
			which acted with Brigade HdQrs.	
BAT.	5th		The two NCOs advanced to BHY and later to FLAMENGRIE in both instances the guns	
FLAMENGRIE			reconnoitred the positions to which they were affiliated.	
			The two NCOs again advanced about 2000x, but no call was made for the services of	
			the affiliated guns.	
	7th	0900	The Battery was relieved on the line by the 57th Light Trench Mortar Battery and	
			on relief marched back to billets in ETH.	
	8th		Orders were received to proceed by march route to FLAMENGRIE. Further orders received	
			en route that the Brigade should reach NAUDIN with all possible speed. Packs and limbers	
			were dumped at FLAMENGRIE and the Battery proceeded with Brigade Hd Qrs to NAUDIN.	
			Almost immediately further orders were received to move to TAISNIERE and the Battery set	
			out for that place by march route at 15.00 hrs.	
TAISNIERE.	9th		TAISNIERE was reached at 16.30 hrs and billets were found close to the Church.	
			Rested at TAISNIERE. The Division was relieved in the line.	

Army Form C. 2118.

WAR DIARY
or
INTELLIGENCE SUMMARY for November 1918

(Erase heading not required.)

Instructions regarding War Diaries and Intelligence Summaries are contained in F. S. Regs., Part II. and the Staff Manual respectively. Title pages will be prepared in manuscript.

Place	Date	Hour	Summary of Events and Information	Remarks and references to Appendices
TAISNIERES	10th		Orders were received to move back to BRY which was reached about 11.30 believed the enemy was pinned on that Route	
BRY	11th	11.00	the hostilities ceased the remainder today's time signal	
	12th		In billets at BRY	
	13th		Orders received to proceed on the following day to VENDRIGIES	
	14th		Moved by march route & rested billets at VENDRIGIES	
	15th		Were reviewed the battery arrived at RIEUX about 11.30 hrs and went accommodated in billets in the Rue de la Grand Place	
RIEUX	16-23rd		Training in steady drill etc	
	24th		Orders received to move by march route to CAMBRAI	
	25th		Moved to CAMBRAI via RAPERIE and HAYNES the arrived the battery was accommodated in billets which we had previously occupied in the Rue de RUMILLY	
CAMBRAI	26th		Battery rested	
	27th		Orders to entrain were received	
	28th	09.00	The Battery entrained and was conveyed by motor bus to TROIS via ARRAS & DOULLENS	
TROIS	29-30		In rest billets at TROIS	Copy CC 52 711 (S)

D. D. & L., London, E.C.
(A7883) Wt. W800/M1672 350,000 4/17 Sch. 52a. Forms/C/2118/14

Army Form C. 2118.

WAR DIARY
or
INTELLIGENCE SUMMARY.
(Erase heading not required.)

Instructions regarding War Diaries and Intelligence Summaries are contained in F. S. Regs., Part II. and the Staff Manual respectively. Title pages will be prepared in manuscript.

Place	Date	Hour	Summary of Events and Information	Remarks and references to Appendices
THOMAS	1/1	8am	Battn billeted at THOMAS	
		10am	Kit inspection	
		11am	Route march. Bat. Hd. Qrs. moved into new billets. No. 6 KILLER'S & Hd Qrs the usual by the left	
		2/1/16	Rose & unit was to billets inspection & cartrige hall in the am	
ROUTA			3/1/16 Route march Battalion ordered out at 9.40 pm	

www.ingramcontent.com/pod-product-compliance
Lightning Source LLC
Chambersburg PA
CBHW081443160426
43193CB00013B/2365